AUTUMN TRAVELS
DEVIOUS PATHS

AUTUMN

POETRY

TRAVELS

& PROSE

DEVIOUS

BY HERMAN TAUBE

PATHS

DRYAD PRESS
Washington D.C. & San Francisco

Dryad Press extends its appreciation to Morris Rodman and Joseph and Martha Mendelson who have helped support the production of this book.

Book and cover design by Sandy Harpe

Published by
Dryad Press
15 Sherman Avenue
Takoma Park, Maryland 20912

Library of Congress Catalog Number: LC 92-52942

ISBN: 0-931848-83-0 (clothbound)
ISBN: 0-931848-84-9 (paper)

ACKNOWLEDGMENTS

We gratefully acknowledge the following publishers for permission to quote from the following works:

Behrman House for *Shloyme Reb Chaims* translated by David G. Roskies and Raymond P. Scheindlin in Ruth R. Wisse *A Stetl and Other Yiddish Novellas of Bygone Days*, 1973.

Crown Publishers, for Binem Heller's poem, "Pesach Has Come to the Ghetto Again," translated by Max Rosenfield, from *A Treasury of Jewish Poetry* by Nathan and Maryann Ausubel, 1957, pp. 273-274.

The Dial Press, for Paul Kresh, Isaac Bashevis Singer — *The Magician of West 86th Street*, p. 297, pp. 3-4.

Farrar, Straus and Giroux, Inc. for Isaac Bashevis Singer, *The Family Moskat*, 1952.

Forward Farlag for Chaim Lieberman *When the World Was Afire* (Yiddish), 1947, vol. II, pp. 548-583.

The Jewish Publication Society of America for *Yiddish Tales*, translated by Helena Frank, 1912: Y.L. Peretz's *A Woman's Wrath*, p. 3, 58 and Sholom Aleichem, *Gymnasiye*, pp. 1-2, 162.

St. Martin's Press for Len Ortzen, *Famous Stories of Resistance*, 1979, pp. 120-127.

Yiddish Scientific Institute - Yivo, for the *Yivo Annual of Jewish Social Science*, Volume I, 1946, Elias Tcherikower: *Jewish Martyrology and Jewish Historiography*, p. 9, 10. Abraham Joshua Heschel: *The Eastern European Era in Jewish History*, p. 2, 87. Dan Miron: *Sholem Aleykhem: Person, Persona, Presence*, 1972.

We also acknowledge the following publications in which essays and poems in *Autumn Travels, Devious Paths* first appeared: *The Washington Jewish Week*; *The Forwerts* (Forward) New York; *Algemeiner Journal*, Brooklyn, New York; *On Hoyb*, Miami Florida; *Israel Nayes*, Tel Aviv; and *Hayotzer*, a publication of the Jewish Folk Arts Society, Rockville, Maryland.

CONTENTS

In Memory of Ruth Indritz — O H

FOREWORD

In an age of specialists, Herman Taube is a man of many literary parts: poet, short story writer, novelist, essayist, journalist, teacher. *AutumnTravels, Devious Paths* is a means to enter into his work and meet those whosm his spirit has kept company with.

Since arriving in the United States from Germany in 1947 with his wife Susan, he has lectured and published prodigiously — in Yiddish and increasingly in English. He may write conversational essays about the Yiddish writers who have had a profound influence on Jewish life and world literature — a selection of these informal articles form the first part of this book. And he may write poems of the deep pleasures of the passing moment, as in "Autumn Sunset" and "Autumn Love." Still, his subject is one of desperate memory: call it the Holocaust, the Shoah, the Churban. It is an obsessiveness which cannot escape the memory of calamity that eliminated millions of Jews in Europe and 500 years of Yiddish culture.

In "Letter to a Poet," he writes, "I am a self-imposed/ codifier of chaos, so preoccupied with pain/ that I am condemned myself/ to solitary exile."

> Writing about the past
> defies all logic, sense
> I'm in a spider web,

entangled in images
who haunt me, hold me,
calling, demanding:
Write! You are our memory.

The past holds Herman Taube in thrall. The stories in the second section of this book are set between the late thirties and the end of World War II. They focus on individual heroism and self-sacrificing devotion in the midst of Nazi Europe, for example, the seemingly mad Leybele who gives the utmost of gifts — his life for another. Or in "Kol Nidre," set in Lodz, Poland in 1939, on the eve of Yom Kippur when Nazis dragged Jews into the street, the frail Rabbi Abraham, the most unlikely of heroes, takes all that the German SS gives him, and in his quiet subversiveness raises his voice in the "Kol Nidre," lifting other Jewish voices, bringing upon himself further beatings, but resisting in the only way it is possible to resist — deep in the recesses where the spirit lives.

In one sense, Herman Taube's stories and poems are a means of containing the memories, giving them a habitation that by doing so, pays homage to them. The process of recreating memory — that is, making the poem or the story — is a rescuing of order out of the disorder. The poem or story is a record of having made some sense out of the chaos of a past whose consequences have been so disastrous.

Every work of art, no matter its subject, is an act of bringing order and, no matter how reluctantly, of affirming life. There is no poem that says no, because there would be no poem. There would be no story, no painting, no sculpture, no act of making, of assembling, of integrating. No writer wants to make art from the Holocaust — that is a sacrilege and an abomination. But there are those writers whose lives have been irrevocably shaped by the Jewish experience of Nazi Germany who cannot help themselves; they cannot and will not forget.

Elie Wiesel wrote of Herman Taube that he "portrays the sad mood as well as the spirit of hope of survivors." This can be said of numerous Jewish writers — Chaim Grade, Primo Levi, Elie Wiesel himself — Herman Taube is the only European poet of his generation who has written such a substantial body of poetry in English. The best of those poems are wonderfully compelling, rich in nuance and in metaphor. This achievement is astonishing when one realizes that he didn't begin to learn the language, let alone write in it, until he was 32 years old. Here is one example. In "At the Peretz Shrine," the poet writes of Pinchas the caretaker of the Warsaw Gensia cemetery, whose sad face reminds Taube of "the synagogue beadle in Peretz's stories." But all that has been destroyed by "the gas chambers of Chelmno and Majdanek."

> Pinchas is ready to cry out for the dead,
> For the living, the wreched, lonely souls
> Of Warsaw's remaining Jews. His small eyes look
> left and right: A man is watching him. . . .

> Questions remain unanswered, his voice — clipped
> Like a pair of wings, is ebbing back to silence.

Listen to that voice "clipped/ Like a pair of wings." A voice that would soar, like the voice of Peretz. This is metaphor astonished at itself.

For those writers who are most compelling, the world is filled with significance. At its best, this is what Herman Taube's work does: it teaches us by the energy of its exploration, by its unwillingness to shrink from the world as it is, by saying yes when there is every reason to say no. Some poets make of this world a tragedy. Others, like Taube, look for every spark of light. It is not that he comes singing a happy song — there is a great deal of sadness in his work. But rising out of that sadness is also a wonderful strength that offers itself to us, to listen and to see.

Merrill Leffler

Autumn Travels, Devious Paths

The sweetest melody your heart can sing,
keep for your autumn hour, not for the spring.
Glad is the blossom-time, with its own tune
and chime: Ah, but the sunset-day sing it away.
                                    Abraham Raisen

The blooming spring of my life
was shaken by thunder of war.
It was sheer luck that brought
me from the devious paths of
bloody European soil to this land.

The shady gloom of the past
was diffused by a new glow,
a long summer of sunlight, hope,
love and visions of a future full
of pleasing sounds of freedom.

Now, my roving daydreams take me
back to the spring of my life.
Autumn travels lead me to the
devious paths of my stormy youth:
The seasons repeat themselves.

Conversations
on Yiddish Writers

❖ ❖ ❖

MENDELE MOCHER SFORIM
(Sholom Abramowitz, 1836-1917)

Mendele Mocher Sforim once said to the historian Szymon Dubnow: "I am also a historian, but from from another cut (another style). When you will teach the history of the nineteenth century, you will have to use my writings in order to describe the way of life of my generation." Mendele was not bragging: he knew that we Jews are a people very scant when it comes to recording our history. "There is no shortage of religious books, codes, commentaries on the scriptures and the Talmud, Responsa, ethical and philosophical works, but when it comes to writing history and chronicles, we just are very inconspicuous," writes Elias Tcherikower.

"In ancient times as now, the pious Jewish World, as if deliberately, ignored in its literature the great dramatic experiences of the people: many a Jewish historian and writer, wishing to study the post-exile history of the Jews, has felt that he was lost in a historical desert." Historian Simon Bernfeld writes that after the fall of Jerusalem, Jews lost all sense of history.

Szymon Dubnow in his *Weltgeschichte* claims that for "the first seven hundred years of Jewish history in Europe we do not possess a single Jewish source (except epigraphy). From the days of Josephus Flavius up to the eleventh century there has been practically no Jewish chronicler — Jews simply failed to record."

We know very little of the beginnings of the Jewish settle-
ments in Europe and have practically no Jewish sources con-
cerning the fate of Jews in the four empires of pre-Christian
Rome, Christian Byzantium, Persia and the Arab Caliphate,
or even Moslem Spain for the first two hundred years. "Jew-
ish historians had to go to solely non-Jewish sources," writes
Elias Tcherikower, "which are alien, frequently hostile and
certainly one-sided. And if it had not been for the Greek and
Christian historians who preserved Josephus in translation,
we should have known nothing of one of the most crucial
periods in Jewish life, embracing nearly four hundred years,
from Alexander the Great to the Destruction of the Second
Temple."

I dwell on the issue of the historical value of the Yiddish
writers and storytellers to prove how right Ernest Renan is
when he states that "even a novel may sometimes be a his-
torical document." The historians — Zinberg, Graetz, Zunz
like Dubnow and others — came to the Yiddish writers and
found in their work a treasury of historical facts, a vast array
of epigrams, allegories and tales unequaled in forcefulness, in
spirit, and passion. They found the soul of the people. Only
in this light can we view the role of Mendele as the Zeide —
the grandfather of modern Yiddish literature.

Mendele's work satirizes the narrow, restrictive world of
the shtetl Jews confined by superstition and repression. He
hoped in his writing to influence the Jewish people to broaden
their outlook, to make Jews and Judaism adaptable to modern
times. His aim was to educate the masses and also to make
Yiddish into a respectable language.

Mendele takes us back to the blote, the dirt and conges-
tion of the shtetl, the struggle between the Baal-Meloches
and Baal Taxes, Sheyne Yiddin and Tzebrochene Yiddin,

Reiche Balabatim and poor Yeshiva students to Senderl the Yiddine and Shlomo Reb Chaims. Mendele tells us: "There were no young girls in our times, only young mothers, brides, and children." If the historian will wonder why, he will find the answer in Shlomo Reb Chaims:

> During the evil decree that Jewish children be taken as recruits, Jews got smart and in a haste, brought their young children under the Chuppa [canopy]. It was fully reasonable: "If you, little shrimp, can be a soldier, then you can also be a newly-wed."

Mendele gave us the hope and despair of a century. He shared the sadness and joy with the readers of his time, and left us a treasury of stories which will live for generations.

Mendele began by writing in Hebrew, in such stories as "Ha "Avot Vehabanim" — "Fathers and Sons." Then he realized that to reach and educate the broad masses, he had to speak to them in the simple language they used everyday — he turned to Yiddish. His first satire on Jewish Community leaders was "Dos Kleine Mentschele" ("The Little Man"), followed by *Fishke the Lame* — one of his great novels about the Jewish poor — *The Shnorer* (*Vagabond's Kingdom*). One of his classics is *Masoes Binjamin Hashlishsi* (*Travels of Benjamin the Third*), the activities, dreams and tribulations of a shtetl dogooder in his search to bring deliverance to his oppressed people. Mendele combined humor and pathos. He criticized and moralized; for him, there were "no holy cows." He left us unforgettable scenes and portraits of Jewish life in the nineteenth century.

Mendele is not without his faults and shortcomings. Baal Machshoves (pen name for Dr. Israel Eliashov, 1883-1924), one of the first and best Yiddish literary critics, accuses him of "too much criticism, a bit of mockery, too much of overly cultivated diction, of drinking pure brew without an occasional drop of water, a poor architect who constructs stories that struggle like a wagon on a bumpy country road." Baal Machshoves continues:

> He writes his longer works episodically, linking one set of events to another in succession, but the construct is not an organic whole; it is just strung together, often reminding the reader only at the very end of some plot scheme long since forgotten.

Mendele had a natural inclination to place double meanings in the speeches of his characters. Except when talking about the homeliest matters, their words would tend to assume larger implications hinting at the condition of the Jewish people in general. When the blind wife of Fishke the Lame pushes another man away and says, "Go on! I'm a married woman, thank heaven, and have someone to take me around visiting," we hear in her words an elegant hint at the general situation of the Jewish people. Such passages are everywhere in Mendele's works. This produces an ambiguity which constantly thrusts the reader from the particular to the general and back again, jarring him and interfering with his pleasure.

Like a true son of his people — who are eternally enamored of the sharp phrase — Mendele has an unfortunate habit of ruining a mood he has striven to evoke with a good deal of care and artistry, all for the sake of some clever epigram. At times the witticism he cannot help making is even a good one, yet inappropriate in the context.

All these faults are such significant elements in Mendele's writing that we would probably never have had his work without them. But the shortcomings of a great talent are worth studying no less than its virtues. In a great writer the spirit of his people manifests itself as if through a magnifying glass — everything seems larger and more pronounced. And if we can achieve some understanding of the sources from which our greatest Jewish writers have drawn both their virtues and their faults, we can then understand something of the soul of the Jewish people with all its virtues and faults.

Here is a sample of Mendele's "sharp tongue," how he sees the contradictory trends in the shtetl:

For some time now my pen has been trapped motionless between two contradictory opinions, like Muhammad's coffin, which is said to be suspended between two magnets. While the one strives to attract it toward the past, the other tries to attract it toward what is happening now in our own time. These two forces are bickering within me like two shopkeepers that jump on the same customer and deprecate each other's merchandise. One says, "G-d save us from the new merchandise and the jewelry that are now fashionable among Jews. Nothing that you see here is genuine. It's all a fraud: silver plated clay, an empty shell; mascara, rouge, and jewels on the outside; filth, dirt, and muck on the inside. Nothing is authentic, nothing has any character of its own; everything is crude, like those dolls that seem to open their lips, beat a drum, blow a horn, sound a cymbal, and squeak, but only thanks to the key that wound up their spring. Forget them: here you have fine antiques, every one the work of our ancestors, and each with its own authentic value. The other one shouts: "Come to me! Look at my merchandise — what do you want with outmoded things from an age that is dead and gone? Do you think you're some kind of medium who can raise the dead?" That's exactly why we are in so much trouble now: Jews are oblivious to the present; they attend only

7

to the past. They can't see where they're going, because they face backward, so they stumble and fall. Whatever they do, at home, in their synagogues, in their writing, they are as though dead, dead while alive, and expecting to live after death. A living Jew is worth nothing, but when he dies he gets a fine reputation, and a fine tomb-stone. The dead are all pure and righteous, munificent and sage; a mere radish or onion turns into a cedar of Lebanon and a sardine becomes a whale as soon as he reaches the cemetery.

Despite Mendele's faults, Baal Machshoves considers Mendele "a great talent who understood the inadequacies of his generation." Mendele polished, purified and simplified Yiddish. Those of you who seek in Mendele the talent of a Franz Kafka, Saul Bellow or Thomas Mann will feel partly lost. But for those who want to penetrate into the depths of the old Jewish ghetto-dweller from Kabtzansk and Glupsk, you will find poetic vision and great satisfaction.

Ruth R. Wisse, calls Mendele's writings, "the most de-tailed study of a Shtetl in all of Jewish literature. Time has virtually come to a stop in his work and only space remains. Mendele records every corner and character in the Shtetl, every nuance of attitude and mood." He made it possible for us today to look back and understand our past, our roots, our Bobes and Zeides.

SHOLOM ALEICHEM
(Sholom Rabinowitz, 1859-1916)

Sholom Aleichem creates the most vivid characters, while expressing a great deal of humanness and pathos; he enables us to see the humor in tragic situations. To his readers he brings a panorama of Jewish life. Having an ambivalent attitude, he recognizes that shtetl life is disintegrating, and that it must; yet he feels that a full life is impossible without its traditional boundaries.

You remember Hodel, Tevye's favorite daughter in what most know as Teyve the dairyman. Changes in the world outside of the shtetl cause Hodel to join her husband, an enlightened politically active student who is imprisoned in Siberia. Tevye is able to psychologically expiate his grief by telling the story to Sholom Aleichem.

Who was this man called Sholom Aleichem, a man who wrote 28 volumes of plays, novels, poems and short stories; a man whose work has been translated into most languages of the world, who has been criticized and praised in 6,000 books, reviews and articles; a man so great that even Tevye der Milchikher from shtetle Anatevka, on the other side of Boyberick, a man who usually conversed directly with "The Almighty," shared his complaints, arguments and most intimate stories of his daughters' misfortunes with him?

For many years Sholom Rabinowitz tried to establish himself as a writer either in Russian or in Hebrew — he did not succeed. Only when he published some comic sketches in Yiddish, did he find acceptance and a warm response as a teller of tales and humorist. The people of the shtetlach, the plain folk, fell in love with him. His writings, a blend of humor and sadness, a mirror of the tragic and joyous happenings in Jewish life, reached to all places where Jews read Yiddish.

Sholom Rabinowitz was born in March 1859 in Pereyaslew, a town in the Poltaver Gubernie — Poltava province in the Ukraine. The family lived in Voronkov, a nearby village, later to become famous as Kasrilevke, where Sholom gained his first childhood impressions of what later became the basis for much of his writing. "Sholom early developed a talent to copy, to imitate, to mimic, to grasp the ridiculous in everything and everyone," writes Charles Madison in *Yiddish Literature*. "This was almost a disease with me," Sholom Aleichem later wrote in his autobiography. His mimicry amused bystanders and embarrassed his parents. "Quick of mind and motion, charged with juvenile wit, blessed with a vivid imagination and retentive memory, he soon knew the life of the townspeople to the minutest detail." The death of his frail mother, and his father's remarriage to a shrewish woman from Berditchev (whose complaints and curses he soon listed alphabetically with great relish, extending it to several pages) hastened his maturity. He attended a Russian gymnasium where he studied secular subjects. At the age of 17 he became a melamed — a tutor in the home of a wealthy provincial Jew in a nearby village. When his employer discovered a romance growing between the tutor and his daughter, Sholom was dismissed. Several months later he became a Kazionney Rabin, a government rabbi in Lugni, a town near Pereyaslew.

There are several reasons why Sholom Rabinowitz adopted the pseudonym Sholom Aleichem, reasons that will give us some insight into the situation of Yiddish in the second half of the Nineteenth Century. To begin with, his father and father-in-law preferred that he write in Hebrew. Secondly, I.L. Gordon chastised him for favoring Yiddish, "a language which is a badge of shame, of the driven wanderer. I have always considered it as the duty of every utchony Yevrey (educated Jew) to see to it that the dialect should gradually disappear from our midst," wrote Gordon. Professor Dan Miron gives us a third reason. Sholom Aleichem wrote a biting satire in the *Dos Yiddishe Folk* entitled "Di Vibores" — "The Elections." "His satire," writes Miron, "did not refer to its victims by name and the provincial town where the elections took place was symbolically called 'Darkness.' Nobody at all acquainted with the affair was meant to fail to identify either place or person involved. Moreover the re-elected Rabiner was none other than Sholom Rabinowitz himself." After "The Elections," Sholom Aleichem wrote a series of satires, "Letters Stolen from the Post Office," and he feared the government censor.

A number of Yiddish writers at this time were hiding under pseudonyms because of the low esteem for Yiddish. Leo Wiener in his *History of Yiddish Literature in the Nineteenth Century* calls it, "a cover for their nakedness with a pseudonymous fig leaf." Yiddish was completely lacking in cultural status, despised as "the mixed and deformed jargon of the unenlightened masses," both by the purist Hebraists (the disciples of the Haskalah movement and its Hebrew Literature) and by the newly assimilated, superficially Russified upper middle class. Yiddish was called "unsuitable for cultural and literary use of lasting value."

The reason I dwell on this subject is to emphasize the

great influence Sholom Aleichem and Y.L. Peretz had on making Yiddish an admired and cultural language, a polished, highly valuable and living literature. Yiddish was improving rapidly during the 1880s and was growing with every new essay, story or satire published by Sholom Aleichem. *Di Yiddishe Folk Bibliotek* — his literary almanac — although short lived, epitomized a new status for Yiddish. Many of the Hebrew writers were attracted to his publication in *Mameh-Loshon*, the Mother Tongue. David Frishman, S. Frug and Y.L. Peretz started new careers in Yiddish, without resorting anymore to pen-names. Like Mendele, Sholom Aleichem was the "chronicler of his time, a very proud Jew fighting against assimilation."

Here is an excerpt from "Di Gas" ("The Street") when Sholom Aleichem returns to his old hometown, after many years, for a visit. Finding himself on an unfamiliar street, with modern-looking houses, he stops a Jew who happens to hurry by: "Reb Yid, Zait Moychel, Zait — zie azoy gut — Be good enough to tell me who lives here, in this big brick house.

> "Oh yes, here lives. . . . Wait, wait, I'll remember presently. Oh yes. It seems that no lesser person than Monastiryov, Yakov Borisovitsh Monastiryov lives here."
> "A Jew?"
> "A Jew."
> "Yakov Borisovitsh?"
> "The same!"
> "Wait a moment. Isn't he Yankl Bereles?"
> "Ask me another."
> "Isn't he the son of Berele Monastrishtsher?"
> "Why don't you ask him?"
> "Now don't be angry with me for asking. Do understand. This Yakov Borisovitsh was a schoolmate of mine. We studied in the same *kheyder*, and he was. . . ."

"But where do I come into all this?"

"But you must understand how important this is to me. After all, a friend. . . . I mean Yankl, Yankl Bereles was my friend . . . and suddenly Yakov Borisovitsh Monastiryov! What use does he have for this 'yov' of his?"

"No offense meant, but will you please leave me alone? What are you? A preacher? God's attorney? What do you want? What are you looking for?"

"God forbid? Have I said anything? Have I made any claim on anybody? I just talk to myself. For heaven's sake: Berele Monastrishtsher. A Jew learned in the Torah, a great philanthropist, comes of an elevated family of *rabonin* [rabbis] and *tsadikim* [Hasidic spiritual leaders] . . . — Suddenly he becomes a Borisovitsh Monastiryov! Yov! Do you see? — Yov!! . . ."

"What I see is that you are either an idler or somewhat of a crackpot, or both."

And the impatient interlocutor flees. Obviously, Sholom Aleichem established himself in this conversation as a good, loyal Jew who, although not necessarily an old-style fanatic, is flabbergasted by the total metamorphosis of his once *kheyder* friend.

Sholom Aleichem gave us novels like *Stempenu*, *Yosele (Nightingale) Solovey* and well-known stories, "From the Fair," "In the Storm," "Wandering Stars," "Der Blutiker Shpas" ("The Tragic Joke,"), "Teyve the Dairyman," "Menachem Mendel." He left us monologues and plays, for example, *The Treasury*, *Shver Tzu Zain a Yid*, *Sender Blank*, *The Grand Prize* and *Tzezait un Tzeshprait (Scattered and Dispersed)* that ran in theaters all over Europe and wherever Jews lived.

Dan Miron, in comparing Sholom Aleichem with Mendele Mocher Sforim, writes, "both of them describe, report, overhear, are made confidants, make humorous comments and, most importantly, edit and publish presumably authentic documents and stories."

Typical characters in Kasrilevke, the home of Sholom Aleichem, are similar to Mendele's "Kabtzansk." In this short passage Sholom Aleichem describes his town:

> The Jewish poor have many names. They have been called the needy, the indigent, the impoverished, beggars, mendicants, and dependents. Each name is uttered in pity or contempt. But they have another name: The Kaserilek. This name is pronounced in a wholly different tone. One says, for instance, My, but I am a Kaserilek. A Kaserilek is not merely a starveling, a luckless fellow: he is, if you please, a poor man not downcast by his poverty. On the contrary, he makes a joke of it!

Sholom Aleichem published fiction to the very end of his life and became one of the great classic writers of our century. He withstood many crises, went bankrupt, finally emigrated to America. He left us a great Yerushe — a heritage. He gave us courage with his spirit, with his humor in the time of the Churban.

Now we see a survival of Yiddish and Yiddish literature all over the world. In Israel, in Europe, in the Americas, publishing houses are busy translating Sholom Aleichem in their native languages. In November 1981, I was in Brazil and Argentina and was pleased to meet with college youth — our conversations were in Yiddish. Mendele, Sholom Aleichem, Peretz, with their talent and love for Yiddish made our Yiddish garden bloom. Beautiful flowers are rising on the horizon. Thanks to Sholom Aleichem, the Jew from shtetls

Yehupets and Kasrilevke, Yiddish literature became known all over the world. And Sholom Aleichem, the Jewish Mark Twain, is still bringing joy to his readers.

Maurice Samuel in *The World of Sholom Aleichem* remarks that the history of the shtetls like the chronicle of Tevye the Dairyman's life is largely one of uniform calamity.

> Yet it is read for laughter by tender-hearted people. Not what happens to Tevye is funny, but how he takes it. We might call him Tevye the unextinguishable. We might add, rather helplessly, that sometimes he puts us in mind of a Job with a sense of humor and without the happy ending, and sometimes of Charlie Chaplin.

Reading Sholom Aleichem's stories, you are stimulated and inspired by his commitment to his folksy characters. My favorite stories, "On Account of a Hat" (translated by Isaac Rosenfeld) and "Hodel" (translated by Julius and Frances Butwin) are examples that show what it means to be a mentsch, a human being and a Jew in pre-revolutionary Eastern Europe.

I find myself drawn to Hodel because her character is so strikingly similar to young Jewish women I knew a half century ago in the shtetlach of Poland, Lithuania and Russia. In this nararative you see the tragic figure of a father deeply loving his daughter, praising her virtues, comparing her to Queen Esther, a father who knows that his daughter is lost to him forever. We see a father-in-law decribing Feferl, his son-in-law, his revolutionary passion, his idealism for building a better world, not only for the shtetl but also for the outside world. "He had the wildest notions, the most peculiar ideas. Everything was upside down, a topsy-turvy. For instance, according to his way of thinking, a poor man was far more important than a rich one, and if he happened to be a worker, too, then he was really the brightest jewel in the diamen! He who toiled with his hands stood first in his estimation."

Tevye shares his thoughts with "Mr. Sholom Aleichem" and reveals to him feelings and emotions that he holds back from his own wife. Tevye starts his monologue:

"I am, as you know, a trusting person, and I never question God's ways. Whatever He ordains is good. Besides, if you do complain, will it do you any good?"

There is something paradoxical between Tevye's light, anecdotal description of the story, his figurative speech, the funny Biblical quotations, analogues that Tevye uses and the depth of emotions expressed in this story. You smile, you laugh, and suddenly you realize that your tears are falling on the pages of the book in front of you. . . . Tevye concludes his story with irony: "And now let's talk about more cheerful things. Tell me, what news is there about the cholera epidemic in Odessa?"

I will conclude with Sholom Aleichem's ethical will, which was read into the Congressional Record in 1916. It has been called one of the great ethical wills in history.

Wherever I may die, let me be buried not among the rich and famous, but among plain Jewish people, the workers, the common folk, so that my tombstone may honor the simple graves around me, and the simple graves honor mine, even as the plain people honored their folk writer in his lifetime.

No titles or eulogies are to be engraved on my tombstone, except the name Sholom Aleichem on one side and the Yiddish inscription, herein enclosed on the other.

Let there be no arguments or debates among my colleagues who may wish to memorialize me by erecting

16

a monument in New York. I shall not be able to rest peacefully in my grave if my friends engage in such nonsense. The best monuments for me will be if my books are read, and if there should be among our affluent people a patron of literature who will publish and distribute my works in Yiddish or in other languages, thus enabling the public to read me and my family to live in dignity. If I haven't earned this in my lifetime, perhaps I may earn it after my death. I depart from the world with complete confidence that the public will not abandon my orphans.

At my grave and throughout the whole year, and then every year on the anniversary of my death, my remaining son and my sons-in-law, if they are so inclined, should say *kaddish* for me. And if they do not wish to do this, or if it is against their religious convictions, they may fulfill their obligations to me by assembling together with my daughters and grandchildren and good friends to read this testament, and also to select one of my stories, one of the really merry ones, and read it aloud in whatever language they understand best, and let my name rather be remembered by them with laughter than not at all....

My last wish and my prayer to my children: Take good care of your mother, beautify her old age, sweeten her bitter life, heal her broken heart; do not weep for me — on the contrary, remember me with joy; and the main thing — live together in peace, bear no hatred for each other in bad times, think on occasion of other members of my family, pity the poor, and when circumstances permit, pay my debts, if there be any. Children, bear with honor my hard-earned Jewish name . . . and may God in Heaven sustain you ever. Amen.

YITZHOK LEIBUSH PERETZ
(1852-1915)

I go with my people. My soul is inflamed
by the glory of their flag and I cry out:
"Jews of all lands and states, unite!
Long and dangerous is the road. Close ranks!"
    from "The Day" (written after the pogroms of 1905)

The trio of the early modern Yiddish writers —
Mendele Mocher Sforim, Sholom Aleichem, and
Yitzhok Leibush Peretz — were the fathers to Sholem Ash, Z.
Segalowitz, Isaac Bashevis Singer, Chaim Grade and others
who emerged from the shtetls of Eastern Europe to the mod-
ern world of literature.

Not only did these three authors catch the hearts of read-
ers with their imagination and legends (*folk-mayses*) but they
evoked the spirit of their fellow Jews, the drabness of the
shtetl weekdays, turning them into *Shabos-Yomtovdige Yidden*
(Shabbat-Holiday Jews). They grappled with all the details of
Jewish life, portraying the poor and the rich, the saints and
sinners, the toilers and exploited. Their writings are of enor-
mous importance for future historians who will search for
sources and try to learn how their forefathers really lived in
the corner of the world we call Eastern Europe. However, we
cannot speak of Yiddish Literature — of Mendele, Sholom

19

Aleichem, Peretz, Ash — without first explaining the origins of the Yiddish language, a literary unknown and obscure linguistic phenomenon to the Western World.

Nineteen hundred years ago, after the destruction of the Second Temple, Jews were dispersed from their homeland, settling in lands throughout Europe and Asia. They practiced their own faith, creating distinctive cultures in the countries where they were allowed to live. While they were often isolated from gentiles, they learned to speak the languages of their neighbors, though they used the Hebrew alphabet to write in those languages. They did this with Greek, Persian, Latin, Arabic, Spanish, Italian, French and German.

As far back as the 4th century, Jews were leading a cultural community life in Cologne and Mainz, in the Rhineland. They purposely did not speak Hebrew, which was only used to study the Bible and Holy Books. While they spoke Middle High German, they wrote phonetically with Hebrew characters, adding words and expressions they gained from the other languages. The isolation of Jews behind ghetto walls for many centuries encouraged the growth of language differences, between the Middle High German and Medieval Yiddish.

In the 12th and 13th centuries, spoken Yiddish was nearly equivalent to Middle High German. This is why it was possible for a Jewish poet like Susskind Von Trimberg (1150-1231) to rise to the highest troubador-rank in Germany. A large number of Yiddish poets, for example, Eshenbach and Vogelweide, composed and sang before kings and feudal lords. Their songs survived because Manesse, a Swiss Christian anthologist, transcribed them from memory into Middle High German.

However, while Middle High German was undergoing transformations, the isolation of Jews behind ghetto walls for many centuries — and the isolation of their language — led to differences between merchant Yiddish and German. In the 15th century, when Jews were expelled from France, Spain and Portugal, and moved eastward to Poland and Russia, their language went with them, which added many new expressions, folklore, songs, idioms and aphorisms. It was in the last quarter of the 18th Century with the Jewish Enlightenment Movement (known by the Hebrew word of *Haskalah*) that Yiddish poetry and literature started to flourish.

There is no question that the most modern Yiddish writer in the last 100 years was Y.L. Peretz who was born on May 18, 1852, in Zamosc, Poland. Reared in a Jewish home where tradition had persisted without change for generations, Peretz longed to reach the wide world beyond the walled, unchanging "stagnant ways" of his ancestors. He rapidly discovered that Jews cannot trust blindly all the revolutionary parties and their promises. Assimilation, following false messiahs, led only to despair. He returned to his roots: to the Jewish spirit, to the Yiddish vineyard, to the wit, the eloquence and the warmth of *Mameh-Loshen*. His first poems were written in Hebrew and Polish, though traveling in the Pale of settlements, his heart opened up to the people of the shtetlach — the villages and provinces.

I might characterize the message of Peretz's prose poetry for our generation by his story "Der Gilgul of a Nigun" ("The Transmigration of a Melody") with the "Gilgul of the Neshome" ("The Incarceration of the Soul"). Peretz teaches us that people cannot split, divide or sever their present from the past, that in order to persevere and build a future, we must stick to our roots. In his real life, the Maskil (Enlightenment movement follower) and Hebrew writer became the fighter for Yiddish, with love for his people, adoring the homeless wanderers: the water carriers, the Hebrew teacher, the tailor, the traveling klezmorim. They all possessed a spark of goodness and Godness — they were all the children of the King of Kings.

He found moral grandeur and truth in the life and faith of the folk masses and started to write in Yiddish. Peretz, the statistician doing a survey about the Jewish population, started to write stories about colorful folkways, behavior and rituals of his generation. While collecting statistical data, he also absorbed every spark of light, every voice of hope and protest, every sign, every lament of despair. He gave us the intimate stories of our ancestors in a series of Chasidic tales, folk-stories, plays and poems which embody a pattern of values to live by until this day.

Peretz transformed *Di Goldene Keit* (*The Golden Chain*) of the past, into a new horizon of our people for the future. In his stories he discovered the source of strength, the secret of Jewish survival. Jewish existence, he saw, was whole and holy under the perspective of his generation and under the aspect of Jewish continuity. As Israel Knox has written, Peretz's achievement was "to enable his generation to pursue their own ideals in light and not in half darkness, to diminish the element of fear and to inspire increased hope for a future yet to be shaped."

Peretz revealed that deeds (*maasim tovim,*) and compassion (*rachmones*) are a higher truth. His stories about "Bontche Schweig" ("Bontche the Silent"), "If Not Higher," "Family Peace," "Sholom Bahyis" and "Mendel Braines" carry a keen sense of rachmones and glimpses of real beauty, nobility, and grace.

Peretz's contemporary Mendele Mocher Sforim criticized and made fun of the Jews of Glupsk, Gniloyadevke, Tuneyadevke. He was saddened by the sight of dirt, hunger of the poor, downtrodden Jews of the Nineteenth Century. But Mendele saw the *blote* (mud) of the shtetlach, the drama of his people's sufferings, sitting on a high balcony. Sholom Aleichem did the same: criticizing, moralizing in a more modern way, *"laughing through tears,"* showing the forlorness, the ludicrousness, the tragic-comic situations and characters of Kasrilevke and Boyberik, Tevye, Menachem-Mendel, Motel — the Orphan, Shimele Soroker, and his Etye-Menye. They all reach deeply into our souls and show us the despotism of the Czars, the wave of pogroms and expulsions ordered and designed by the Czarist regime.

But Peretz is different from Mendele and Sholom Aleichem. Peretz also makes adverse comments about Jewish habits, through *remozim* (allusions) and *mesholim* (fables); he also goes to Glupsk, but not to measure the mud, but to seek out the Jewish spirit laying low *in der blote*, and what a beautiful treasury did he discover. In his story "Drei Matones" ("Three Gifts"), Peretz brings to light an old man, beaten by the soldiers, lashed with their whips. When the old Jew who is bleeding reaches the end of the row, he notices that he lost his yarmulke. Without hesitating, he walks back through the line of the soldiers to pick up the yarmulke and covers his head.

In his story of "Avreml Bass" the not-too-clever would-be fiddler, who is always laughed at for playing in disharmony, the unpolished musician, while playing at a wedding with other Klezmorim, has the bow fall from his hand and he drops dead. The Rebbe announces that Avreml Bass's death was not an accident — "it was so decreed from above, because the heavenly orchestra lacked a bass-player and of all conceivable candidates Avreml Bass was chosen to fill out and perform with the heavenly orchestra." One of the most famous of Peretz's tales is "Tzvishen Tzvei Berg" — "Between Two Cliffs." The discussion between the "Bialer Rebbe" and "Brisker Rav" gives us the essence, the soul of Peretz's writing:

23

Jewishness is not confined just to the pages of the Holy Books, but it embraces the whole world, people, trees, the sky, the sights of smiling faces, the sound of laughing children. . . . My Rabbi, your Torah is the soul for Klal Yisroel.

In his essay "Our Platform," Peretz writes:

We do not want other people to stand aside at harvest time and to weep over lost years on the day of rejoicing or to beg for alien bread to which will cling the sweat and toil of alien peoples. We also want to bring a bit of corn and wheat into the common granary. We also want to be partners, junior partners, but not beggars. We want the Jew to feel that he is a human being, participating in all common human activities, living and striving like a human being, and — if insulted, reacting to insults like a human being.

This is the legacy Peretz left to us, a message to Jews who retreat, run away from Judaism and Jewish values:

What is Jewishness? Jewish heritage? Jewishness is the Jewish way of looking at things. Jewishness is the universal spirit as it is embodied in the Jewish soul. Jewishness is what makes the Jews, in eras of national independence, feel free and enables them to fashion institutions as embodiments of their national creative will. Jewishness is in such times: joy, ecstasy, zestful living.

Nachum Sokolow describes the *mentsch* Peretz as:

An active, dynamic human being, always smiling, friendly, not stingy. His home — open for everyone —

his food, his clothes he shared with the needy. He was a good lawyer and gave of his law services, very often, free.

A warm host, he liked to do a "favor." A man of talent and a man of deeds. A *Schtub Zitzer* — a man who liked to stay home, yet with his spirit and vision he saw the world from end to end.

Peretz was active in many relief committees. He was the co-founder of a society with the unusual name, "The Cholera Committee." Actually, this was a society for relief for homeless Jews running from pogroms and poverty, a committee that organized free kitchens, gave free food parcels and arranged shelter for the homeless. The Committee existed for many years.

The "Geminah" — where Peretz worked, was the central office. This was a regular "Federation" with volunteers, a women's division which delivered meals to the poor and homeless. Peretz gave a lot of his time to this committee, visited the affluent Jews of Warsaw for what we call now "face to face solicitations." He involved the leaders of the Geminah.

Sholom Aleichem reminisced about his visit with Yud Lamed Peretz in the spring of 1915, the last week of Peretz's life, and the reception given for him in *Hazomir*, the artists and writers club where Y.L. Peretz was President, their walks in the streets of Warsaw, their chats and dreams about going to Palestine: They were dreaming, planning to go to Palestine "to see, to think, to tell later what we will see with our eyes and feel in our hearts, walking on the soil from where our roots are coming, where all our spiritual heritage, our prayers and hopes are directed to." But it wasn't destined for Y.L. Peretz to visit Palestine with Sholom Aleichem. On April 3, Chol Hamoed Pesach, 1915, Y.L. Peretz died while writing a poem.

For those of us who were raised and still dwell in Yiddish literature, the writings of Yitzhok Leibush Peretz, poet and prose writer, allegorist and romanticist, still occupy a supreme, unique hold on our spirit. Yud Lamed Peretz, the master of neo-Chassidic stories, folk tales and a blend of social-moral drama seventy to eighty years ago still evokes a truly religious ecstacy today, seventy-five years from the day when the one hundred thousand Jews of Warsaw followed the procession of his funeral from his home on Cegelniana Street to the Gensza Cemetery.

I have visited OHEL PERETZ, Peretz's monument, three times: in the spring of 1938, in the summer of 1945, and in the fall of 1975. On my first visit, I had to walk for a long time the short distance from the entrance of the cemetery to the OHEL. Thousands of people from all over Poland and from many countries filed by the OHEL PERETZ, where the Father of Yiddish Literature and his two close friends S. Ansky and Y. Dinezon are buried. Slowly, in a procession, people were carrying flowers, singing Peretz's songs and chanting prayers.

When I read the inscription on the tombstone: "In azoy gehen mir zingendik un tantzendik" — "So, we shall go along, singing and dancing, we great, great Jews. Sabbath and festive Jews," I did not feel a mood of sadness or loneliness. Everything around this place was full of a hypnotic spirit of Peretz and his heroes: The Brisker Rav, the Bialer Rebbe, everything here, from the beggars who lined both sides of the alley leading to the OHEL and the mass of admirers and followers were singing in unison:

> "For each his own life, for his
> babes and his wife,
> For himself and the house of
> his father."

Leaving the cemetery, I was in the midst of a vibrating, active community of over four hundred thousand Jews. The influence and inspiration of Peretz was living among them. There were many productions of his dramas: *The Golden Chain* and *Night at the Old Market Place.* There were fifty Jewish libraries in Warsaw, as well as Yiddish schools and clubs named after Peretz. Hundreds of bookstores displayed new editions of his popular folk stories.

The Jews of Warsaw, despite poverty, discrimination and enormous hate propaganda against them, and despite traditional anti-Jewish prejudices existing there for many generations, were working, building, trading, traveling, praying, singing, reading books, learning Torah, fighting for their daily survival and Peretz' songs were with them.

From many an open window, I could hear the rhythm of sewing machines and a voice of a girl singing Peretz's "The Three Seamstresses."

> The needle gleams the linen snow.
> One thinks to herself, I sew and sew,
> I sew by day and at night I sew,
> But no wedding dress for me, oh no,
> What is the use of my sewing?
>
> There is no food and no sleep for me.
> I would give a few pennies for charity,
> That G-d in recompense maybe
> Might send an old widower for me,
> Even with a host of children.

In June 1945, I returned to Warsaw to find the city destroyed, the Jews of Warsaw destroyed in the Ghetto, exterminated in Treblinka, Majdanek, Chelmno and many other concentration camps all over Eastern Europe. The last 40,000 Jews of Warsaw died on the barricades in the Rising in the Ghetto, from April 19 to May 8, 1943. Only a small group of heroes survived and were sent to fight against the Nazi oppressors with the partisans and resistance groups in the ghettos of Cracow, Czenstochov, Bendin and Bialystok.

I was in the uniform of a Red Cross worker in the Polish Army and the people at the railroad station were very polite, pleasant and willing to help me, to accompany me through the ruins of Warsaw to the Jewish Cemetery.

At OHEL PERETZ, I found half of a quorum of Jews, former soldiers in the uniforms of the Polish and Russian Armies. They were transferring decomposed bodies of Jews found in the rubble of the destroyed city to the mass grave a few hundred yards from the Peretz monument. I tried desperately to control my emotions: Oh Peretz! What happened to our Shabbos-Yomtovdike Yidn? Where is your Nemirover Tzadik? What happened to your Wonvolitzer Rabbi with his songs and dances "serving G-d every hour of the day with his body and soul?" Who is singing now "The Talner Melody?" Where is your "Beryl the Tailor" and "Yochanan the Teacher?" Their bodies are ash and dust! Soap for German hausfraus and fertilizer for the fields of Eastern Europe.

I left the cemetery and walked aimlessly through the ruins of the Ghetto. Beside me walked my guide, an elderly Pole, who pointed out areas and blocks around the cemetery.

"Your people and our people were victims of terrible persecutions here. The Nazi occupants destroyed this precious city. They desecrated your synagogues and our churches. We lived through tragic years. Your people were real fighters here . . . house to house, bunker to bunker. They had no chance for victory. Still, they were fighting. We sent them all the assistance we could . . . arms, food . . . unfortunately, we did not succeed."

We walked back to the railroad station. I paid the guide and left the city of Peretz's dreams with my soul dead. No hope, no belief in justice, in mankind, nothing!

In October 1975, thirty years and six months later, I returned to the Peretz monument in Warsaw. I went with a United Jewish Appeal mission of fifty-five fellow Washingtonians to Poland, Romania and Israel, as witnesses of the Holocaust. The city of Warsaw was rebuilt, the uprooted population returned from labor and concentration camps in Germany and in Russia to start a new life under a new system. In 1975, Warsaw's population reached the same number of citizens as in 1939: one million two hundred thousand people, except the four hundred thousand Jews who never came back. There are in the area of Warsaw only a few hundred Jews, remnants of the Holocaust, or survivors of Russian prison camps.

Again, I am at the OHEL PERETZ. This time, no more Shabbos-Yomtovdike Yidn. Not even "Wochendike Yidn," except for one elderly caretaker, Pinchas.

We walked past an alley of crumbling, broken stones, past the graves of great rabbis, artists, teachers, famous Jews and Ghetto fighters. Rabbi Mathew Simon recited prayers, Susan Snyder read Peretz's poem, "Believe Not":

> Believe not that the world is for naught, made
> For the wolf and the fox, for murd'rer and cheat;
> That the sky is a blind to keep God from perceiving
> The fog that thy hands not be seen
> And the wind just to drown bitter wails.
> The world is not hovel, market or cast-off.

All will be measured, all will be weighed
Not a tear nor a blood drop will fade.
Nor the spark in one soul be extinguished uncharged.
Tears gather in streams, and streams into oceans.
Oceans will swell to a flood.
And sparks burst into thunder . . .
Oh, think not there is not judgment or judge!

Cantors Lester Tepper and Donald Weisman chanted the El Mole Rachamim. We all said *Kaddish* and again the Gensza cemetry heard a reading in Yiddish, Bialik's "In the City of Slaughter":

Arise and go now to the city of slaughter,
Into its courtyard wind thy way;
There with thine own hands touch, and with the yes of
thine head
Behold on tree, on stone, on fence, on mural clay,
The spattered blood and dried brains of the dead.
Proceed thence to the ruins, the split walls reach,
Where wider grows the hollow, and greater grows the
breach;
Pass over the shattered hearth, attain the broken wall
Whose burnt and barren brick, whose charred stone
reveal
The open mouths of such wounds, that no mending
Shall ever mend, nor healing ever heal.

We left the OHEL PERETZ and stopped for a moment of silence at the grave of Mordecai Anilewicz, Commander of the Warsaw Ghetto Uprising. The skies of Warsaw were gray that morning. Sam and Regina Spiegel walked beside me looking at the last remaining part of the Ghetto Wall due to

be torn down to make room for a children's playground. . . .
Regina Spiegel asked a question: "What will happen to this
five hundred year old cemetery after the few remaining
Pinchases are gone? "What will happen to the OHEL PERETZ?"

We walked in silence; I was thinking: As long as we live,
Peretz's writings will live among us. All we need is hope. We
will go to Israel, will return to America, and there we are still
singing Peretz's "Hope":

> Hope! Not distant is the Springtime,
> Butterflies will soon be winging
> In new nests the merry songsters
> Their new songs will soon be singing.
> Know! The night itself will vanish,
> Cloudlands drift and melt away
> Once again will skies shine azure,
> Stars by night and sun by day.
>
> New the roses, new the flowers,
> Spring's new odors flow in waves
> Brilliant colors, scents and singing
> Will rise above our graves.

ISRAEL JOSHUA SINGER
(1893-1944)

"**M**y late brother I.J. Singer," wrote Isaac Bashevis Singer, "author of the *Brothers Ashkenazi*, was not only my older brother, but my spiritual father and master as well. I looked up to him as a model of high morality and literary honesty. Although a modern man, he had all the great qualities of our pious ancestors." In the numerous stories that Bashevis Singer published in the *Jewish Daily Forward*, he always mentions his brother with gratitude, as a friend and teacher, and a man whose path he followed. His brother died in 1944 at the age of 51, leaving a huge number of stories, dramas and novels. Best known are *Earth's Pain, New Russia, Steel and Iron, Yoshe Kalb, Spring, Comrade Nachman, The Karnowski Family* and *The Brothers Ashkenazi*.

I.J. Singer's literary force is his capacity for vivid, graphic description. He has the subtle and sharp eye of an analyst who can tell a simple story and faithfully portray his characters — the Jewish people of Poland. His story "Pearls" made him famous in the domain of Yiddish literature and his novel *The Brothers Ashkenazi* as well his many short stories are classics of Yiddish literature.

In his stories he is more than an observer — he walks along with his heroes in difficult situations, in their anguish, in their wars and revolutions. He penetrates not only their

33

actions in great detail, but enters the depth of their souls. We follow his heroes and become involved in their struggles, in the Russian Civil War or during German occupation. For those of us who study our history we must turn to I.J. Singer's novels to better understand the struggle and growth of the modern Jewish community in Poland during the first half of the twentieth century. I remember when *Yoshe Kalb* was produced on the stage in Lodz, Poland, before World War II. Despite the protest by Orthodox Jews, thousands came to the Yiddish Theater — his play was an honest protest against customs and manifestations in Jewish life.

In *Yoshe Kalb* Singer painted a picture of nineteenth-century Jewish life in Galicia, Austrian Poland: the Neyesheve Rabbi Melech wants to marry off Serele, his dull-witted teenage daughter to Nahum, the frail, fidgety son of the somber, outstanding and famous Rabbi of Rachmanivke, in Russia — so that he himself will be free to marry his fourth wife Malkah, an orphan girl. Despite the opposition to the match of Nahum's mother, the wedding is arranged. Singer describes in detail the intrigues, the heady excesses that lead to the wedding ceremony: the pale, scared and shy bridegroom is terrified when he is left alone with Serele in the bridal chamber. Petrified Nahum cries for Mama when Serele moves toward him awaiting her fourteen-years-young husband to perform what is needed to consummate the holy union. Soon afterward Rabbi Melech weds the neurotic, irritable Malkah who refuses to shave her head and withholds her body from her husband. She goes from one tantrum to another until she develops a passion for Nahum. Malkah seduces Nahum in a moonlight forest.

On her way to the rendezvous with Nahum, she snatches a candle from a lamp in a barn; she flings it into a heap of straw while making love with Nahum. The Nyesheve synagogue goes up in flames and burns down to the ground. When Malkah dies bearing Nahum's child, he leaves town. His wanderings take him to the village of Bialogura, where he gets a job sweeping, fetching wood and drawing water for the synagogue. They call him here Yoshe Kalb — Yoshe the Loon. He gets involved with the beadle's daughter Ziviah, a fleshy woman who shares willingly her lust with any man who asks for it. She gets pregnant and Yoshe is blamed and forced to marry her. Soon afterward he flees the town and fifteen years later returns to Nyesheve to his Serele. But the Bialogura tribunal catches up with Yoshe and he is tried. The tribunal asks: Are you Nahum, Serele's husband, or are you Yoshe, Ziviah's husband?

A wise man of the village answers, you are Nahum and you are Yoshe: You are a scholar and you are an ignoramus. You appear suddenly in cities and you disappear suddenly from them; you wander in the cemeteries in search of your own kind and you steal through fields at night and wherever you come you bring with you disaster, terror, pestilence. You unite yourself with women; you flee from them and you return. You don't know what you do; there is no taste to your life or in your deeds, because you are nothing yourself, because, hear me, you are a dead wanderer in the chaos of the world. . . .

The next day, Nahum-Yoshe disappears from Nyesheve, now indeed a dead soul and wanderer. The Orthodox community of Poland was outraged by this play and the negative reaction to the dialogues by young theatergoers. But the play made Singer world famous. Even those who did not agree with his treatment of the main characters enjoyed the style of his writing. Singer guides Yoshe the Calf with love and sympathy against corruption, against abuses, against the distortions that affect us.

Singer's great novel *The Brothers Ashkenazi* about Lodz, the city where I lived the first two decades of my life, was the most popular novel in Poland before World War II. It opens with the wandering Jews from Silesia and Saxony traveling the sandy roads into Poland, "through townlets and villages laid waste by the Napoleonic Wars." The breadth of the narrative introduces us to characters, some positive, some repulsive, trying to establish new roots on Polish soil.

The only one in Lodz who wouldn't yield to the commandant was Tevye, the leader of the unionists and chairman of their executive committee. Each order the baron issued, Tevye countermanded. In the middle of the night his cohorts fanned out with buckets of paste and rolls of proclamations, which they proceeded to glue over those signed by the baron.

Baron Colonel von Heidel-Heidellau flushed an apoplectic scarlet when he learned of the nocturnal depredations. "Wipe them out without a trace!" he frothed at Police Commissioner Schwanecke. "Crush the Jewish vermin responsible for this!"

The lame commissioner marshaled all his men to lie in ambush for the perpetrators. He also sent out spies and agents to trap them. A few were collared, and he personally kicked them in the belly, venting all the rage and humiliation he had been forced to endure from the baron.

He used all his policeman's wiles to learn the names of the group's leaders, but the prisoners wouldn't talk even when he starved them. Schwanecke then proposed they spy for him, but they wouldn't go along. Finally, he sent them into forced labor in Germany.

He had proclamations posted explicitly defining the punishment meted out for covering or defacing German orders, but the same night the executive committee managed to cover all these proclamations with their own calling for an ongoing struggle against the army of the occupation and its lackeys the police.

The war between the baron and Tevye had been triggered by food. As one way to supply more food for the fatherland, the baron had turned to the workers' soup kitchens. A committee of Lodz's elite, including Yakub Ashkenazi, had maintained these soup kitchens, where the workers could get a bowl of thin gruel and a crust of bread. But even though the support for this effort came from the Lodz citizens themselves, the baron cast a covetous eye upon the enterprise.

They consumed a lot of staples, these soup kitchens — mounds of potatoes, flour, and groats that might have better gone to Germany — and the baron summoned the leaders of the citizens' committee to his palace and ordered them to add more chaff to the flour used for the bread.

"Excellency, the bread is already falling apart from all the adulterants in it," the leaders protested.

"Add the ingredients my senior medical officer suggests, and the bread won't fall apart," the baron said. "I'm not allocating any more flour for your rabble, and that's that."

When the men tried to explain that the substitute bread was making the population sick and spreading epidemics, the baron lost his temper. "There is plenty of ground to bury all the people of Lodz!" he roared. "Get out!"

With great realism Singer shows us the Ashkenazi family and the Jews of Lodz. Skillfully he absorbs the smoke of the industrial city and the soul of Lodz Jewry in their struggle for survival and is honest in describing the social struggle for survival and the political struggle of the Jewish workers for justice. Aaron Zeitlin called Singer "a spiritual realist who dared not accept changes in the world order at the expense of the individual, a poet and painter of human destiny."

Born on November 30, 1893, in Bilgoraj, Lublin District, Poland, Singer's father was the Rabbi of Lentchitze (Lynczyce). Young Singer studied in Yeshivot and Beth Midrashim and until the age of 17 he did not know how to write an address in Polish or Russian. He learned Hebrew calligraphy and became a copier of Torah scrolls at the court of the Rabbi of Radzimin.

At the age of 18, he arrived in Warsaw and went to school. He started to read the literature of the Maskilim — the Enlightenment. Yud Lamed Peretz helped this forlorn, provincial lad, advised him in his homework and his first writings. But Singer was not sure if he wished to be a writer. He dreamed of becoming a painter — he met the famous Polish-Jewish painter Maurice Trembatch, who invited him to his attic room. Singer saw the poverty and hunger and how Jewish artists lived. When he shared with Trembatch his dreams, the great artist sarcastically exclaimed, "Why do you want to be an artist? Look at me, look at this attic room, all I live on is a menu of potatoes." Singer then tried everything: photography, drawing, writing, teaching Hebrew, office work, manual labor. He was hungry and desperate, he slept in attics and thought of suicide. The experiences of the hunger years prepared him, like Maxim Gorki in "My Universities," for his literary vocation. He developed a style of writing without adornment — direct and open. Here is an example from "Repentance" (translated by Maurice Samuel).

"Repentance?" shouted Reb Ezekiel, and his voice was as gay as if he had heard the sweetest tidings. "Repentance?" Assuredly! Take a glass of brandy. What is the meaning of the word "repentance"? It is: to turn! And when a Jew takes a glass of brandy he turns it upside down, which is to say, he performs an act of repentance.

And without waiting Reb Ezekiel filled two silver beakers with brandy in which floated spices and little leaves. "Good health and life, Reb Naphthali," he said and pushed one beaker forward.

Reb Ezekiel emptied his beaker at a gulp. Reb Naphthali broke into a stuttering cough at the mere smell of the drink, but Reb Ezekiel would not let him put it down. "Reb Naphthali, you have come for my counsel. The first thing which I will teach you will be the mystery of eating and drinking."

He forced Reb Naphthali to swallow the brandy and then pushed toward him a huge piece of stuffed carp, highly seasoned. "This," he said with a smile, "comes from the hand of my wife. She is a valiant woman, a pearl of price, and her stuffed fish have in them not less than one-sixtieth of the virtue and taste of Leviathan himself."

The first piece Reb Naphthali tried to swallow stuck in his throat. But Reb Ezekiel would not be put off, and he compelled Reb Naphthali to eat. "Rabbi Naphthali, the road of repentance is not an easy one, as you see. But there is no turning back on it."

When it was impossible to make Rabbi Naphthali eat another bite, Reb Ezekiel took him by the hand, led him into the other room, and bade him stretch out on the well-stuffed leather-covered couch.

The stormy years of the Russian Revolution he spent in Kiev, working for a newspaper and as a manual laborer on the waterfront on the Dniepr docks. Singer observed the Russian Revolution from the near, from the inside, and what he saw was disappointing to him as the established Czarist order, before the revolution. He returned to Poland in 1921 and published his story "Pearls" in a Warsaw newspaper. Abraham Cahan of the *Jewish Daily Forward* reprinted the story and offered Singer the position of the European correspondent for the *Forward*.

After the success of his novels *Steel and Iron* and *Yoshe Kalb*, he emigrated to the United States with his wife and son. America was good to him; so were the critics who compared his works to Tolstoy's. He wrote much: stories, plays, novels, and essays. The more he wrote and studied, the more he felt how bankrupt the modern world is. He began to dream and write about Eretz Yisrael and wanted to write a book about Bar Kochba. He called the Galut (the Diaspora), "The Two Thousand Year Mistake."

He bought a set of Talmud "to refresh all he forgot" and started searching for his roots. Spiritually he returned to the world of his father, The Rabbi, a velt vus-iz nishto mer, a world that is no more. Aaron Zeitlin reminisces about Singer: "A day or two before the high holidays I found him singing high holiday melodies, one after another . . . he could not stop. This was an expression of longing for a lost way of life. Singer the realist became romantic — Er Hot Ge'Benkt Noch A Velt Vas Iz Mer Nishto."

In his works, Singer came to the tragic conclusion that the individual is condemned to lose in any society, totalitarian or democratic; that history shows all dreams and accomplishments of the individual finally succumb to the will of society. Regardless of his momentary gain of success, in the final count he is only a number, a snow flake in the snowstorm of life. He loved deeply and sensually the individual, and he felt the human tragedy. He saw firsthand how a revolution under the slogan "Bread and freedom for the individual, actually destroyed everything he possessed." In *The Brothers Ashkenazi* Singer concludes:

If a pack of mad dogs attacked a man, was there any reason for the victim to feel degraded? Dogs were stronger than man, but they remained dogs, and man remained a man. The Jews of old had had the right idea. They held the gentile in such deep contempt that his insults and derision meant less to them than the bite of a mosquito.

No, it didn't pay to give up one's life for such foolishness. The strength of Israel lay not in physical force, but in intellectual superiority, in reason. Since time immemorial, gentiles had persecuted, mocked, and oppressed the Jew, and he had been forced to keep silent because he was in exile, because he was a helpless minority, a lamb among wolves. Could the lamb then oppose the wolf? . . .

Had Jews adopted the gentile's ways, they would have already long since vanished from the face of the earth. But the Jews had perceived that theirs had to be a different course, and it was this perception that had lent them the moral strength to endure and to accumulate the only kind of force the gentiles respected — intellectual and economic power.

This was the strength of the Jew and his revenge against the gentile. Not with the sword, not with the gun, but with reason would the Jew overcome. It was written: "The voice is Jacob's voice, but the hands are the hands of Esau." The Jew lived by his reason; the gentile, by his fists. For hundreds of years Jews had danced to the gentiles' tune because they were too few to resist. In times of danger the Jew was obliged not to sacrifice his life, but to appease the wild beast in order to survive and persevere.

Singer died in the middle of his creative life. His legacy for Yiddish literature lives on among us and was carried forward by his brother Isaac Bashevis Singer, a great writer whose work pulsates with love for Yiddish and whose talent has reached many nations and many literatures.

ISAAC BASHEVIS SINGER
(1904-1991)

I went to the rabbi to get some advice. He said, "It is written, better to be a fool all your days than for one hour to be evil. You are not a fool. They are the fools. For he who causes his neighbor to feel shame loses Paradise himself." Nevertheless the rabbi's daughter took me in. As I left the rabbinical court she said, "Have you kissed the wall yet?" I said, "No; what for?" She answered, "It's the law; you've got to do it after every visit." Well, there didn't seem to be any harm in it. And she burst out laughing. It was a fine trick. She put one over on me, all right.
"Gimpel the Fool"

Isaac Bashevis Singer, a former Yeshiva student, emerged in the literary circles of Warsaw with a knowledge of secular subjects and modern Hebrew and familiarity with Kabbalah. Growing up in Warsaw in a poor home and poor neighborhood on Krochmalna Street, his father held a Bet Din, a Rabbinical post of judge, arbitrator, advisor and marriage counselor.

From the beginning, Singer was a prolific writer, his imagination inhabited by demons, corpses, and devils. The winner of many distinguished literary prizes, he was awarded the 1978 Nobel Prize for Literature. His writing has been characterized as paradoxical, sentimental, realistic, supernatural and mystical.

He hovers constantly between princesses and peasants, the pious and sinners, the rich and the starving. He strolls with ease from the shtibl, the Chasidic prayer house, to the house of sin. Corpses long buried in Europe walk around alive and well in Miami and New York.

Yakov the slave, who lived centuries ago in the time of Bogdan Chmielnicki's pogroms, survived the Holocaust and we see him in a shtetl somewhere around Lublin in 1948. (Or was it in the Bronx among his enemies?) Bashevis's life may be more paradoxical than his writings: a sceptic by nature, he is constantly searching, questioning, doubting everything except God. "The fact that I exist is a mystery to me," Singer has written. "I live, I walk on mysteries. Look at the Bible. The Bible is not obscure, it is wonderfully clear."

He has been attacked by the orthodox and many traditional Yiddish writers for his obsession with sex. Bashevis answers them, "I believe in God, but, I don't believe that God wants man to run away completely from pleasure. If he has created men and women with a great desire for love and to be loved, there must be something in it, it cannot be all bad."

The attacks on Singer bring to mind a legend about a swallow and King Solomon. Legend has it that King Solomon, tired by the nagging of his thousand wives, escaped to the solitude on the roof of the Tower of David, desiring a few moments of rest and silence. He looked at the Judean mountains; with fascination and love, he inhaled the cool clear Jerusalem air, and the desired peace and quiet came to him. Suddenly he hears a pair of hovering swallows engaged in love making and having the following conversation: "Who is this Solomon, anyway?" the male swallow was asking his mate, "What are all his palaces and armies worth? If I wish I can destroy all his towers with one stroke of my wings."

Solomon, who could understand the languages of animals and birds, could not ignore such anti-monarchy talk. In a severe tone he ordered the swallow to present himself and account for such a boastful statement. The swallow replied as follows:

"Oh wisest man, great Solomon, where is your common sense? Don't you know that lovers like to exaggerate when they wish to impress their sweethearts?" Solomon smiled and sent the bird back to his mate, who was waiting in fear on an eave of the tower.

"Oh please, tell me what did the great Solomon want from you?"

"The King," answered the swallow, "begged me to show compassion on him and not destroy his towers and palaces."

The swallows of modern day literature accuse Bashevis Singer of exaggerating about his sexual powers in order to impress his many sweethearts — his readers.

Like Sholem Asch, Singer has been praised by many gentile critics and attacked by conservative Jewish writers. Yet, the swallows believe him, read his books and love his stories. Yiddish newspapers have printed pages of articles and critical essays attacking Singer with rage. The attacks might be likened to a Shin Shalom novel *The Light Did Not Go Out*. The hero Zofnat is harrassed by an elderly Jew with a white beard and long, black kaftan, who comes to Zofnat's home in the middle of the night to enjoy a promise given to him by the Tzaddik of Karlin — Zofnat's grandfather. The Tzaddik promised him to live to see and dance at Zofnat's wedding. Zofnat, a poet and writer immersed in plays and literature, is single, a man without a skullcap, not even a mezzuzah on his door.

The Chassid is flabbergasted: "Do you know who you are?" he asked Zofnat. "When you were born, a great festivity was proclaimed throughout your father's court. You are a descendant of the Rizhiner, a "Yoresh" of Pshische, a grandson of the "Seer of Lublin" — the Choze of Lublin. You could have brought redemption to the nation of Israel, and I find you without a skullcap writing stories and poems."

Shin Shalom's story and the articles of the Yiddish press are tailormade for Bashevis Singer. Knowing Isaac Bashevis Singer and the great influence Y.L. Peretz has had on his writing, I think I know the answer Bashevis would give to his attackers, "Why he, a Rabbi's son, left the Yeshiva to become a Yiddish writer." I will quote from Peretz's story, "Two Cliffs":

Tell me, Noah, why did you escape from our yeshiva?

Rabbi, I was short of breath, I wasn't able to breathe.

How come? What are you saying, Noah?

Not me, my soul was breathless. . . .

Why Noah?

Your Torah is full of judgment, without mercy, without a spark of kindness is your Torah, therefore she is without joy, without free breath, pure iron and brass, iron punishments, copper laws and very high learning, good only for the elected chosen . . . Tell me, Rabbi, what are you doing for the general public? for the woodchopper, for the butcher, for the workingmen, for the simple Jew?

Rabbi, I have to tell you the truth: Hard was your Torah, hard and dry, because she was only body and not the soul of the Torah.

The soul? asked the Rabbi of Brisk.

Sure! Your Torah is only for the chosen, for scholars, not for the masses; learning must be available for all

46

our people. Holy inspiration is hovering over all our people, who study our Torah — the soul of Am Yisroel. . . .

Isaac Bashevis Singer the Yeshiva student decided to bring enjoyment to the masses. His parents' roots helped him to better understand his past, but for Singer, past is present. *The Slave*, for example, deals with a story three centuries ago, though it is also a novel of post-war Europe, a picture of our own generation. *The Slave* is not just fiction of Singer's imagination — we find many similiar stories in our history. Here is an entry from the diary of prince Jan Ducklan Ochotsky:

January 5, 1874. The Innkeeper Hershko did not pay his rent for the last season, 91 thalers, and I arrested him together with his wife and family. I keep him locked up in the pig house. Only his boy Leizer, I took in my house and force him to study the New Testament and Christian Prayers. The boy is very bright and handsome, I hope to convert him. He refused to cross his heart, but Streletzki gave him a good beating and today he already eats pig meat. With help from the Priest we hope to overcome the stubborness of this boy." (Szymon Dubnow, foreword to *Die Geshichte das Chasidismus*)

Similar episodes in our history go back many centuries. Jews were sold, enslaved, exchanged like cattle by land owners up to the second decade in the Twentieth Century. *The Slave* is set in the immediate aftermath of the Chmielnitzki Massacres — actually you see the chain of the Holocaust tragedies of our vanishing world.

To understand Bashevis's writing, look at his literary philosophy: "In Literature as in dreams, death does not exist." Someone asked Bashevis Singer, "Do you believe in the resurrection of the dead?" His answer, "They never died." For six

47

decades he explored dreams, fantasy, passion, imagination. In one story, "The Admirer," he writes: "At times I go to bed with these fantasies and they are transformed into dreams, I see towns full of movement. I hear Yiddish spoken. If I didn't know that these places had been destroyed, I would go to see if everyting matches my dreams." In "Old Love," he writes about one of his heroes: "In his dreams, his three wives were still alive, and so was his son, Bill, and his daughter Sylvia. New York, Warsaw, his hometown in Poland, and Miami Beach merged into one. He, Harry, was both an adult and a school boy."

Singer's stories, recurring in New York, Miami, Buenos Aires or Tel Aviv, are always a version of Poland — a version of Singer's youth. His dreams and memories carry the reader there. This includes *Enemies: A Love Story* and a number of short novels like *Hanka, A Tale of Two Sisters, A Pair*, all of which have major references to the Holocaust. Singer portrays the modern, free, individualistic man as being alone, bored, brooding, restless. With only a meaningless presence he is always on the verge of surrendering his freedom, the void of his life, to the promise of some new meaning. Eziel Babad of *The Manor* and *The Estate*, Heshel (Herman) Bannet of *The Family Moskat*, Herman Broder of *Enemies* — they are all, while thinking themselves free, in reality wavering between two slaveries. Unwilling to accept the Gods of the modern world or unwilling to return to the God of their fathers, they are like Yasha Mazur, "The Magician of Lublin," walking a tightrope.

Freedom, Singer argues, cannot serve as an end in itself. Man needs to be anchored in something more substantial than his own, very precarious self; he needs to bind his own individual life to something larger and more lasting. Man's problem is not a simple problem of freedom, but the great dualistic paradox of freedom and slavery: he can achieve genuine freedom only when grounded in a genuine slavery. What constitues genuine slavery? For Singer, it was the beginning of the realization that man is indeed rooted in something which transcends him — a people, a God, a history. "You cannot ignore history," writes Singer, "The past is as alive as the present." This rooted belief would later appear as the unifying thread of the story of Jacob of Josefov, the slave. Singer's accidental brush with the past gave him a taste of continuity and permanence, of a relationship between the present moment and the timeless, between the life of the individual and the eternal. As the years went by and he became increasingly disenchanted with modern civilization, he would find himself escaping to Bilgoray, his shtetl. "My future," says Singer, "is my past." In this he was exactly like his brother Israel Joshua.

Singer's slavery shapes his life and his work and gives both a sense of purpose. In novels, short stories, essays, and plays, he meticulously records the history of his people.

> I often feel like a man who was given many treasures but has neither the time nor the possibility of making use of them. Sometime I feel that our people, the living and the dead, call me from all sides to do justice to their great lives and unusual deaths. . . . I get up every morning with the feeling of excitement of a man who must do more than is in his power . . . . I would not call myself the last Yiddish writer, but I am certainly one of the last. It is both a tragedy and a responsibility.

The writer, Singer teaches, like the man, is shaped by a particular experience; he is enslaved to a particular vision. But his slavery does not confine him: it is through his slavery that he achieves his freedom. If Singer proves one thing, it is this great paradox: the closer and truer the writer and the man remains to this particular experience and vision, the closer and truer he is to universal experience and vision. On the one hand Singer's world is bound to Jewish emancipation and enlightenment in Poland; on the other, it is bound neither by time nor by place. In his story "Gimpel the Fool," Singer deals with superstition and human cruelty in our own backyards:

> I was coming home from school and heard a dog barking. I'm not afraid of dogs, but of course I never want to start up with them. One of them may be mad, and if he bites there's not a Tartar in the world who can help you. So I made tracks. Then I looked around and saw the whole market place wild with laughter. It was no dog at all but Wolf-Leib the Thief. How was I supposed to know it was he? It sounded like a howling bitch
>
> When the pranksters and leg-pullers found that I was easy to fool, every one of them tried his luck with me. "Gimpel, the Czar is coming to Frampol; Gimpel, the moon fell down in Turbeen; Gimpel, little Hodel Furpiece found a treasure behind the bathhouse." And I like a golem believed everyone. In the first place, everything is possible, as it is written in the Wisdom of the Fathers, I've forgotten just how. Second, I had to believe when the whole town came down on me! If I ever dared to say, "Ah, you're kidding!" there was trouble. People got angry. "What do you mean! You want to call everyone a liar?" What was I to do? I believed them, and I hope at least that did them some good.
>
> I was an orphan. My grandfather who brought me up was already bent toward the grave. So they turned me over to a baker, and what a time they gave me there!

Every woman or girl who came to bake a batch of noodles had to fool me at least once. "Gimpel, there's a fair in heaven; Gimpel, the rabbi gave birth to a calf in the seventh month. Gimpel, a cow flew over the roof and laid brass eggs." A student from the yeshiva came once to buy a roll, and he said, "You, Gimpel, while you stand here scraping with your baker's shovel the Messiah has come. The dead have arisen." "What do you mean?" I said. "I heard no one blowing the ram's horn!" He said, "Are you deaf?" And all began to cry, "We heard it, we heard!" Then in came Rietze the Candle-dipper and called out in her hoarse voice, "Gimpel, your father and mother have stood up from the grave. They're looking for you."

To tell the truth, I knew very well that nothing of the sort had happened, but all the same, as folks were talking, I threw on my wool vest and went out. Maybe something had happened. What did I stand to lose by looking? Well, what a cat music went up! And then I took a vow to believe nothing more. But that was no go either. They confused me so that I didn't know the big end from the small.

In his novel *Shosha* is Singer's attempt to deal with individuals and personal tragedies of people in the years preceding World War II. His central character Aaron Greudinger is torn by love affairs with many women, with the actress Betty, who is willing to take him to America, still he marries his childhood sweetheart Shosha and remains in Warsaw. In *Shosha*, Singer has Greudinger say, "I believed that the aim of literature was to prevent time from vanishing."

In a later part of the book Singer writes, "How is it possible after all, that someone should simply vanish? How can someone who lived, loved, hoped and wrangled with God and with himself, just disappear? I don't know how, and in what sense, but, they are here, since time is an illusion, why shouldn't everything remain?" Twice I asked Bashevis Singer why don't you write about the Holocaust; his answer was, "I wasn't there. I am not worthy to write about it." But Singer, in *Enemies* and in *Shosha*, makes his contribution to our past. His writings prevent our shtetl and our people from vanishing. This is his greatness. Singer writes: "For me the Jews of Eastern Europe, specifically the Yiddish-speaking Jews who perished in Poland, for me they all are living right now."

At a ceremony of Jerusalem's Hebrew University where he received an Honorary Doctorate, Bashevis Singer made the following statement: "Yiddish is not only the language I speak, I also dream in Yiddish. In literature as in dreams, death does not exist. In dreams everything is alive. I will write in Yiddish even if — God forbid — I will be the last Jew to speak the language. But we are not so far yet. Yiddish will remain the eternal heritage of our people, like Hebrew and Aramaic. We Jews suffer from many diseases, but amnesia is not one of our maladies. Our memory is strong and eternal."

Several years ago, the Jewish Community Center of Greater Washington staged his play *Yentel*. I was the "literary consultant." On the opening night of the play I spoke to Singer, and told him that 50 young people are now reading his books. He was pleased and happy to hear this. He said, "Yiddish will continue in Yiddish and in translation for many generations, in many places. The Jewish spark, the Jewish soul lives and will live. Don't worry Taube, Abi Gezund, you can see that even in a Washington there are young Jews who like to read and see plays by a Yiddish writer."

In August 1990, I attended Yiddish classes at Bar Ilan

University in Ramat Gan. There I met students from Kiev, Bucharest and Frankfurt, who came to study Yiddish in Israel. There is a revival of Yiddish in what was the Soviet Union and in Israel. Over 3,000 students study Yiddish in 57 schools in Israel. Dr. Gershon Wiener, Dean of Jewish Studies at Bar Ilan, spoke of the great demand for Yiddish teachers for Eastern Europe. In Israel, a new edition of the works of Sholom Aleichem, Peretz and Singer, just published, was sold in three months.

At a ceremony of the annual presentation of the Yitzik Manger Prize at the Museum of the Diaspora in Tel Aviv, over 400 people came to listen to the Yiddish writers. There are Yiddish courses in many universities in the United States, Canada, England and South America.

Bashevis was correct when he said, "Yiddish is old, weak but not dead. We saw in our century the miracle of the resurection of Hebrew. It can also happen with Yiddish. Why not?"

❖ ❖ ❖

Isaac Bashevis Singer

We met in forty eight, in a cafeteria
on East Broadway. My friend I. Metzker
introduced us: This is the world-renowned
Yiddish author Isaac Bashevis Singer.

You asked me about Lodz, my family,
the war years and about Susan, my wife.
I told you how much I enjoyed reading
your two-volume novel, *The Family Moskat*.

I must have said nice things about your
brother I.J. Singer, his story, *Pearls*,
and his great novel, *The Brothers Ashkenazi*.
Two years later you gave me the novel.

On my visits to your home you always spoke
of your brother, about his life and works:
Yoshe Kalb, *The Karnowski Family*, "Spring."
Bilgorei was closer to you than New York.

I was with you in Chevy Chase, Maryland,
when you received the news that you were
awarded the Nobel prize for Literature.
The prize belongs to Yiddish, you said.

Last time I spoke to you in Miami, Florida,
you said: Remember Reb Meshulam Moskat?
"Hakol Hevel — he says, all is vanity.
My goal was to keep Yiddish alive. Nu?"

You were more concerned about Alma, your wife
than your own health: Without Alma I am lost.
I spoke of students' fascination with your books.
You asked, Will we see a resurrection of Yiddish?

CHAIM GRADE
(1910-1982)

C haim Grade is one of the most important poets and writers in contemporary Yiddish Literature. The son of Rabbi Shlomo Mordecai Grade, one of the leaders of the Vilna Maskilim and a Hebrew scholar, Chaim walked "all the way" in his fathers footsteps. While he believed in Haskalah, he held to his roots, to an abiding loyalty to his faith and to his people. Every group claimed him as their own. Because of his Yeshiva background the Orthodox considered him a loyal Jew; because of his secular poems the Communists wanted him in their *cheder*. But Chaim searched for his own road, sought his own truth and followed his own way.

When Grade was still a boy, his father suffered through a crippling disease and died. He and his mother were reduced to a devastating poverty, living in a tiny hovel that was part of a blacksmith's shop in a courtyard over-filled with other Jewish families struggling to survive. The mother, Vella, peddled fruit at the court-yard gate. With Grade's young wife, Frumme-Liebche, a nurse and herself the daughter of a famous rabbinical family, Vella died at the hands of the Nazis when they overran Lithuania at the outset of their invasion of Russia.

My Mother's Sabbath Days was Grade's last book, a memoir translated by Chana Kleiserman Goldstein and Grade's widow, Inna Hecker. It is a memorial primarily to Vella's piety, courage and perseverance through a hard and tragic life. It is filled with tender reminiscences and remembrances of a Jewish mother who deserved a better life than the one she had, but who never questioned her lot. It is about this book I want to speak.

Grade himself survived by escaping into Russia just ahead of the advancing Germans. In Vilna the belief was that the Nazis would not harm women or children, but would force the young males into slave labor or execute them. When Grade said goodbye to his mother and his wife, he was convinced, as indeed they were, that they would be safe. Yet, as he traveled deeper into Russia, going as far as Tadzhikistan in central Asia, he knew he would never see them again. His grief over their loss is pervasive throughout the book.

My Mother's Sabbath Days is divided into three sections: The first is an account of Grade's life with his mother in their Vilna Ghetto; the second describes Grade's flight from the Nazis, the plight of the Jewish refugees fleeing eastward, and life in the "Communist paradise"; and the third concludes with Grade's return to Vilna with its depopulated burned-out ghetto. His conclusion is an eloquent "Yizkor," a moving tribute to his own losses and to the end of the great center of Jewish learning and religious devotion that marked Vilna before the Holocaust as the "Jerusalem of Lithuania." Powerfully evocative, Grade's closing chapter "Ne'ilah" describes his need to come to terms with the apocalyptic events of his life and to find the will to go on living.

As impressive as all this is, it would not distinguish Grade's work from a host of other compelling accounts of the Holocaust suffering. Where Grade's writing differs is his enormous capacity for bringing a multitude of marvelous characters back to life. In addition to Vella, Alterka, the goose-dealer, and Lisa, his wife who courts the rich; Nossen-Nota, the synagogue Gabbai, who berates the shopkeepers for not closing the shop early before shabbat begins; the ill-tempered, embittered humpbacked Velvel the tailor; Hayka the Maiden, the ghetto's tramp; Rasputin, the chief schnorrer, with his seven wives; Zalman Press, the henpecked stock-peddler and Reb Refoel, the silent taciturn second husband Vella marries on the eve of the war. The people Grade encountered in transit, on the road, in the forest, on the crowded flatcars moving into the Russian hinterland, and in central Asia, and the handful of survivors who, like himself, are drawn to Vilna after the war, come back to life, to whirl around in our consciousness.

Accompanying the remarkable evocation of character and enhancing it is Grade's lyricism. His prose is always poetic, and his talent rises to the demands of the intensely emotional experiences he is recording. Perhaps it is this aspect of his writing that is thoroughly captivating. There is an orchestration of feeling, of repetition, of linkage here that is charged with a powerful organic sensitivity.

Longing

She's so thin, she's so small,
She barely reaches my shoulder,
But in her pain and her mourning
She's grown taller than all.

Mother mine! Gray little dove, dear,
With eyes full of meekness and fear,
In wind and in darkness I lie

And I sing you a lullaby.
On my breast rests her head,
I wipe off her tears as they flow,
As with her sweet fingers she strokes
Beads of sweat from my brow.

I hear from afar her faint moan:
"You shall endure all, my only son!"
On her dear face I count each furrow:
"Die not, my Mother, from longing and sorrow!"
                        Translated by Inna Hecker Grade

Here are a few quotations from "My Quarrel with Hersh
Rasseyner," Grade's story about his confrontation with a reli-
gious Jew who castigates Grade's turning away from strict
adherance to the law.

"How estranged you feel from all secular Jews can be
seen in your constant repetition of 'we' and 'you.' You
laugh at us poor secularists. You say that our suffering is
pointless: we don't want to be Jews, but we can't help it.
It would follow that the German made a mistake in
taking us for Jews. But it's you who make that mistake.
The enemies of Israel know very well that we're the
same; they say it openly. And we're the same not only
for the enemies of Israel, but for the Master of the World
as well! In the other world your soul won't be wearing a
cap or a beard or earlocks. Your soul will come there as
naked as mine. You would have it that the real Com-
munity of Israel is a handful of Hersh Rasseyners. The
others are quarter-Jews, tenth-Jews — or not even that.
You say that being Jewish is indivisibble, all or nothing.
So you make us Jews a thousand times fewer than we
already are.

"Reb Hersh," I pleaded with him, "look at those statues. Come closer and see the light streaming from their marble eyes. See how much goodness lies hidden in their stone faces. You call it idolatry, but I tell you that, quite literally, I could weep when I walk about Paris and see these sculptures. It's a miracle, after all. How could a human being breathe the breath of life into stone? When you see a living man, you see only one man. But when you see a man poured out in bronze, you see mankind itself. Do you understand me? That one there, for instance, is a poet famous all over the world. The great writer broadens our understanding and stirs our pity for our fellow men. He shows us the nature of the man who can't overcome his desires. He doesn't punish even the wicked man, but sees him according to his afflictions in the war he wages with himself and the rest of the world. You don't say he's right, but you understand that he can't help it. Why are you pulling at your beard so angrily, Reb Hersh?"

He stared at me with burning eyes and cried out, "For shame! How can you say such foolish things? So you could weep when you look at those painted lumps of matter? Why don't you weep over the charred remains of the Gaon of Vilna's synagogue? Those artists of yours, those monument-choppers, those poets who sang about their emperors, those tumblers who danced and played before the rulers — did those masters of yours even bother to think that their patron would massacre a whole city and steal all it had, to buy them, your masters, with the gold? Did the prophets flatter kings? Did they take gifts of harlots' wages? And how merciful you are! The writer shows how the wicked man is the victim of his own bad qualities. I think that's what you said. It's really a pity about the arrogant rebel! He destroys others, and of course he's destroyed too. What a pity! Do you think it's easier to be a good man than an adulterer? But you particularly like to describe the lustful man. You know him better, there's something of him in you artists. If you make excuses for the man who exults in his wickedness, then as far as I'm concerned all your scribbling is unclean and unfit.

Foremost is Chaim Grade, a Mekinon, a lamenter of his dor — his generation. His voice, like Elie Wiesel's, is the voice of the third of the Jewish people silenced by the Holocaust. His poems are a lament of a wounded generation lost, surrounded by enemies, silent onlookers, alien neighbors who did not care. Grade is at home not only with Jews of Vilna, of Lithuania and Poland; he is intimately, remarkably engaged in all internal conflicts in Jewish life. His sensitive soul is penetrated by the pain of the survivors and their struggle to rebuild their lives.

I remember him on a visit with us in Baltimore. We sat hours past midnight listening to him speak with anxiety and affliction about Zalam Shazar, about Israel, about the Jewish community in the Soviet Union being destroyed spiritually and about his friend Abraham Sutzkever. His lecture at the B'rith Sholom Hall in Baltimore was eloquent, cool, to the point, wonderfully phrased. But in the three hours after the lecture that we spent together, all the hidden hurt confined in his heart came out. He talked about disunity in the Jewish world, how we foresake the struggle of Russian Jewry, the same way part of American Jewry foresaked European Jewry during the calamity of the Holocaust. He called on us not to give up the struggle.

I look outside: is there a sign of daybreak?
The melancholy blue nags at my heart.

I must pull through this all to sleepless nights of heartache
And with a mighty Yea! the new day starts.

Shall my heart which neither brave is nor believing
If need be forcibly command; Believe!

Grade came to the United States in 1948 and lived in New
York with his second wife Inna Hecker until his death in
1982. Three novels, *The Well*, *The Yeshiva* and *The Aguna*,
and the collection of novellas, *Rabbis and Wives*, have been
translated into English. His poems were forged in the fur-
naces of annihilation and suffering, they were written with
blood and tears of his brothers and sisters — the martyrs and
heroes of Vilna, Lublin, Kiev: "Let my eyes gather-in all that
consumed/ in flame and their memory will endure." Grade
asked: "Who perhaps knows why my dove has perished?/ Why
is the field still green, why are the birds still soaring?"

Grade, as all who have survived, gave no reply to this
question. The nightmares pursued him, his hurting, terrified
soul, his heart burnt like Thomas Mann, like Ruziewitz, like
Paul Celan and Primo Levi. Niger, in an article about Grade's
novel *Refugees*, asked why Grade the former Yeshiva student
was not more traditional, religious, humble. He answers, be-
cause he is the poet of a rootless generation who wanders on
the naked road in a morally-naked world among cities that
have been destroyed physically and spiritually. How can he be
polite, humble and religious? In his poem "To Life I Said
Yes," Grade writes:

My brother in peril, the sun declines.
Like a flame on an altar it is burning.
We have trusted our hopes to the mountains,

And an outstreteched arm is a wing.
The mountain top is yearning for the blue,
Two shapes in the snow towards the summit are turning.
Up! We shall await there the hour
Like trees waiting for leaves in the spring.
                    Translated by Joseph Leftwich

And in "My Mother," he writes:

The cheeks collapsed and the eyes half-shut,
My mother listens as her knees sigh:
The whole morning under the winter sky
She ran about to every market.
So let us now at the gate of the wall
Sleep through the night . . .
And her hand cries:
A bird too gets exhausted from fluttering about
As its wings rise and fall . . .
And her head sinks down—
But my mother flicks the daydream off,
Like a tree shaking off the rain.

Her face smolders, a fire pot,
Her hands measure, weigh;
She pleads, she calls,
Till again she dozes with eyes half-shut;
Her hand taps at the freezing air
And stays there, streteched-out.

Just like
A shadow on the snow,
She sways back and forth the whole day long,
Until late night;

She rocks reself like the pointer of her scale,
To the left, to the right.
Hunched-up, one large hump,
She rots in the snow flurries,
Like the apples in her basket —
And sleeps . . .

Her cheeks glow like coals,
Her neck is whipped by the sleet.
Wrapped up in wind and snow
My mother sleeps standing on her feet.
And when the market snores like a grisly black hound,
She gathers her baskets,
Like a beggar his pennies,
And the market's red eye is put out.
But right at the threshold her steps start to weep:
Wasted hope!
Worn out, she stumbles through the hut
And sleeps.

The lantern hiccups in her hand,
Choking with smoky tears.
She rocks at the wall
As in front of a grave,
And sleeps.

The ax lurks in her hand,
Above her twisted fingers,
And the fiery tongues of the little stove
Menace her wrinkled cheeks —
And she sleeps.
She forgets to take out her hands:
They are freezing in the kneading bowl.

Her thin shoulder shakes,
She washes, she trembles with eyes cast down,
And she sleeps.

When at last the pot between her knees,
The spoon to her mouth,
Again her hand falls down,
Exhausted and slow
She falls asleep —
My mother sleeps . . .

AARON ZEITLIN
(1899-1974)

"Nothing will avail You in the least You have done everything to make me renounce You, to make me lose my faith in You, but I die exactly as I have lived — a believer!"
"Yossel Rakover's Appeal to God" by Zvi Kolitz

In 1752, a Christian scholar, Professor L. Christaner, wrote, "Mit Yiddish ken men oysforn a welt" — with Yiddish you can travel the whole world. But in our generation, after the calamity of World War II, after the destruction of 2,500 Jewish communities in Europe, this is no longer so.

After the loss of a third of our people in the Holocaust, not much was left of Yiddish creativity in Europe, except psychological scars, a sense of futility: Tzu wos? Far wemen? Yiddish, which lost most of her readers in Churban Europe — in Yiddish Churban refers to the Holocaust — became the bereaved, desolate orphan among our people. The reborn State of Israel, struggling to establish a country with a language that would unite her newly arrived immigrants, looked at Yiddish as a symbol of Galut, the diaspora. Some called Yiddish a loshon bezuya, a stumbling block, and too competitive with the aims and goals of the reborn nation. Only in the United States, Argentina, Canada and France did Yiddish regain her prewar forcefulness and generate with her new creativity a literature that influenced a whole generation of Jewish writers like Maurice Samuels, Irving Howe, Saul Bellow, Philip Roth, Bernard Malamud, Chaim Potok and Herman Wouk. A very important influence on American-Jewish writers was the teacher and prolific lyricist Aaron Zeitlin.

With his comprehensive vision, his volumes of essays, his poems, his plays *Yaakov Franck, Yiddnshtat, Estherke, Brenner*, his novels *No Man's Land* and *Brenendike Erd*, he deeply affected the hearts of his readers, students, and the younger generation of writers in America, Europe and Israel. Zeitlin emphasizes the determination of an individual to hold on to his roots, to his faith, to his belief in Ahavat Yisroel:

> Being Jewish means running forever to God
> even if you are His betrayer,
> means expecting to hear any day,
> even if you are a nay sayer,
> the blare of Messiah's horn;
>
> means, even if you wish to,
> you cannot escape His snares,
> you cannot cease to pray —
> even after all the prayers,
> even after all the "evens."
> *Translated by Robert Friend*

Zeitlin's writings lend themselves to classroom analysis — they contain and are based on historical happenings in Jewish life. "Our past," says Zeitlin, "is our inheritance. Even the revolutionaries among us who would like to change things, they are also inheritors: When they fight against our 'old ways,' they recognize that this inheritance is also theirs. To feel the present, the here and now, without our past, is artistically impossible."

Aaron Zeitlin's plays were successfully performed and well received by European and American audiences before and after World War II; like his poems, they are a median between the experiences of our people and his private voice and vision. He was a master of the Yiddish and Hebrew poem; the poem "Names of Jewish Children," for example, shocks us with the velocity of the images of the Moyshelech and Sorelech, a million and a half of them that perished in the Holocaust. His poems possess qualities and expressions full of drama; his didactic narratives swell with sadness and despair, but also with hope: "I cannot conceive," writes Zeitlin "choosing not to believe in Him who, having turned my body to fine ash, begins once more to wake me." Zeitlin's life is firmly interlocked with the life of his generation. "The rhythm of his poetry to the rhythm of his peers," writes Israel Biletsky, "from its very beginning it carried a warning that Jewish life on the banks of the Vistula was built on tottering foundations."

Zeitlin is the master craftsman who combines in his works the conventionality of Yiddish folk slang with the symbology of our past. His writings lift the reader to a spiritual high — they stick to our soul for months and years after we read them.

Aaron Zeitlin was born in Bowaritch, White Russia, in 1898. He was the son of the great Jewish philosopher, mystic and writer Hillel Zeitlin o"h, who perished in the Holocaust. He started to write in a period after World War I, when Jewish life turned into a paradoxical enigma. According to historians like Arnold Toynbee, Jews were fossils, destined to disappear from the world map. After the Holocaust there were questions, even among Jewish scholars and writers, about how Jews could still remain Jews after all that befell us. Aaron Zeitlin, like the contemporary Yiddish writers of this century, proved that those prophesying doom of the Jewish culture were wrong. After the dark period of the Holocaust, Zeitlin and his colleagues started to write again. His works found their place on the reading list of world literature, even though the work in Hebrew and Yiddish is mostly the expression of a child weeping after his lost family, his people. His poems are a rebellious outcry demanding from God mercy and justice. Justice for the Jewish people who perished, among them his wife and child, his father and family. "God," he cries out, "Return my generation!"

Aaron Zeitlin published his first book of poetry in 1922, a volume called: *Shotens ofn Shney* (*Shadows on the Snow*) as well as a lengthy poem in Hebrew, *Metatron*. In 1926 he became literary editor of the Warsaw Yiddish paper *Undzer Express*. After a number of his plays were staged in the theaters of Europe and the Americas, Maurice Schwartz invited Zeitlin to come to the United States for the premiere of one of his plays — this visit saved his life, though all his family was to perish in Europe.

He became Professor of Literature at the Jewish Theological Seminary, contributor to the Yiddish *Morning Journal* and to a number of Yiddish and Hebrew papers and magazines in Israel, Europe and the United States. His novels *Brenendike Erd*, *Nili*, *Between Fire* and *Deliverance*, and his essays and critical discourses on philosophy, religion, the Holocaust and world literature have had a profound influence on his readers and a generation of students. In "Six Lines," Zeitlin writes:

I know that in this world no one needs me,
me a world-beggar in the Jewish graveyard.
Who needs a poem, especially in Yiddish?

Only what is hopeless on this earth has beauty
and only the ephemeral is godly
and humility is the only true rebellion.
                        Translated by Robert Friend

Zeitlin is unique among the Hebrew and Yiddish poets of our century, Abraham Koralnik has written. Not only are his themes or his religio-mystical concepts Jewish but the sharp Talmud-like distinctions that zigzag through his poems, the exactness of his phrasing, the nuances, the feverish hairsplittings, all are astonishingly brilliant.

H. LEIVICK
(December 9, 1888 - December 23, 1962)

*"For each man is a musical instrument, and the life of man is a
song, and when he completes his song it flies out of his body and
this song — that is, his soul — joins anew the great chorus before
His Blessed Seat."*

Y.L Peretz

I n the poems and writings of H. Leivick, the spirit of Y.
L. Peretz was resurrected. In 1915 Peretz, the father
of Yiddish literature, died in Warsaw; in 1916 Leivick's "In
the Snow" appeared in the anthology *East Broadway*, a series
of poems that established his reputation almost at once. These
poems about the Russian Steppes and Siberian prisons dem-
onstrated his deep understanding of human suffering in the
struggle for freedom.

Leivick's visions of redemption dominated and influenced
Yiddish poetry in the period of two world wars, two revolu-
tions, the Holocaust epoch and the rebirth of the State of
Israel. From his first drama *Die Keiten fun Meshieach* (*The
Chains of Messiah*), written in Minsk prison, to *Die Chasene in
Fernwald* (*The Wedding in Fernwald*), written in 1949 — forty
years later — Leivick gave us dramas and poems that envision
the sanctification of the human spirit.

"In Treblinka bin ich nit geven" he makes demands on mankind and on us Jews to avoid false messiahs, to build our lives on the precepts of social justice and ethical principles. As Benjamin and Barbara Harshav write in *American Yiddish Poetry*, the voice of his poems is marked by "sublimated suffering, messianic fervor, a mystical tone, and a naive humanism combined with a Neo-Romantic musicality . . . imbued with Russian symbolism."

In all of his dramas, even after the Holocaust, Leivick continues his universal search for deliverance: to shelter the chains of slavery, he dreams of a world when

> The whole of the land is open,
> Boundaries, swords — no longer,
> No more rich nor poor
> More faith in man, ever loftier man.

He acknowledges his belief, *ani maamin*, in the victory and sacredness of the human spirit to overcome anguish:

> Ich bren un Ich bren un Ich wernisht farbrent
> Ich hoyb zich oyf wieder un shpan awek weiter.
>
> I burn and I burn and I am not consumed
> Again I raise up and go ever on.

Leivick the visionary figure of modern Yiddish poetry was born in White Russia in the town of Ihuman, near Minsk. In his youth in 1906, he was sentenced to six years imprisonment for revolutionary activities; for belonging to the Bund, he was sent into permanent exile to Siberia. With help he escaped Siberia, making his way across Europe, and sailing for the United States where he arrived in 1913.

Through his drama and poetry, psychological verse narratives and prose, the theme of suffering, human dignity and redemption, writes Irving Howe, "runs like a channel of blood." With the Holocaust as part of our lives, Leivick's poems written before now seem visionary and prophetic. If the camps haunted him to his final days, so did hope and the belief in humanity. In *Die chasane in Fernwald*, as Hirsch sews the wedding gown for the bride, he declares, "Just as the Jew received the Torah after the Egyptian bondage, so must he, today, after Dachau, receive a life, for as the Torah is holy so is the life of Jews holy, and possibly holier."

This is H. Leivick's message to us Jews of the post-Holocaust era: "How good that Jews can still believe and hope,/ How good that Jews despair not in the face of/ Poverty and bereavement."

In a Yiddish class at the University of Maryland, a student Elisheva Cahan translated one poem from the cycle of "Poems of the Yellow Patch."

Honor the Yellow Patch

> I held in my hand
> A piece of yellow cloth
> Wrinkled and crumpled like a rag
> And with a frown and a shudder
> From out of my mouth was forced,
> "This is it — the Jewish yellow badge."
>
> And it came to me in a flash:
> Between each wrinkle was a blue point —
> Six blue crooked points in the shield of David
> And a lump came up in my throat
> Followed by a rush of blood and the exclamation,

"This is it — the Jewish Blue Honor."
And as I suppressed my anxiety
Something cried out over me
And like a storm-wind it knocked me down
And afterwards through the night until morning
I felt a burning in my hand
As if I had touched its soul.

An honor, whose points are crooked
An honor, whose wrinkles encircle
The arms and the stooped shoulders:
And honor which soaked in like a sponge.
Holocaust, sacrifice, and pogroms —
Spread out your love on the yellow patch.

As another student wrote, "H. Leivick takes a simple piece of yellow cloth and gives it a soul, makes it shine like a star in the sky, makes us proud to identify ourselves with the yellow patch, with our people's past and future. Shame of yesterday becomes a proud expression of dignity today. In reading the poem, we all acquire something we did not possess a week ago. We feel more spiritually enriched; each line, each stanza, each word we remember is ours for years to come, to enjoy, share, repeat, and remember. A poem is like a garment — we must wear it, use it in order to enjoy it. People must see it to admire it."

Leivick identifies himself with all humanity. He writes, "All faces bear my features,/ In each one's eye — my glance/ My sorrow — in the heart of every man." He never lost that belief, that longing, that dream of a better world. Leivick followed Shlomo, the character of Peretz's *Die Goldene Keit* (*The Golden Chain*) who refused to pronounce the Havdala

— the benediciton dividing the sanctity of the Sabbath from the weekday doom and daily struggle and sacrilege. Shlomo calls for everlasting Sabbath. Reb Shlomo revolts, so does Leivick. He calls out, "The songs of joy are not yet genuine joy,/ The songs of wonder are not yet genuine wonder."

Genuine wonder is the striving for redemption for humanity, the struggle for freedom and the sanctification of the human spirit. Leivick's was the voice of conscience of our people. He left us a precious legacy of lyrical poems, plays and essays, yes. But he left us more — a missionary zeal, an *ani maamin* for our generation. How to live by the precepts of social justice, how to continue the struggle for freedom and how to find redemptive purpose through inner unity and love for humanity.

❖ ❖ ❖

To H. Leivick

> *All faces — bear my features,*
> *In each one's eyes — my glance,*
> *My sorrow — in my heart of Every Man*
> H. Leivick

I carry your "Yellow Patch" carved in my breast
"The Golem's Dream" penetrated my soul.
What I didn't learn from your poems and dramas
I acquired by listening to your son Daniel
and your daughter-in-law Ida, my dear friends.

Your dramas and poems are the voice
and conscience of my suffering generation.

Your ideals of the sanctification of human life
are the hope for humanity: The road to redemption.
When reading your poems, I believe emancipation is near.

GLUECKEL OF HAMELN
(1646 - 1724)

Yiddish literature, born in a time of Jewish helpless-
ness, in a period of mass expulsions and wanderings,
became a source of solace; it offered relief to the sufferings of
our people during dispersion in Europe and helped them to
endure and survive. In its beginning this literature brought
enjoyment to the masses with songs, plays and Bobe-Mayses
— the fantastic, incredible tales — started by Elijah Levita in
his "Bove Bukh." Yiddish literature became the power that
united Jews on many continents in times of social upheavals,
revolutions, pogroms, hasty transformations in our religious,
economic and national life. Like the Yiddish language, Yid-
dish literature, contains the spark — Dos Pintele Yid, of
Netzach Yisroel — of Jewish survival. When you study Yid-
dish literature, you will find a strong permanent bond be-
tween individual creativity and the collective experience of
Jewish communities in the works of their authors.

Yiddish literature also served as a codifier — a historian
of its time, it became the witness of Jewish history. Yiddish
writers and poets can be compared to Ba'ale Tefilah — can-
tors, some in a small congregation, some in large temples and
synagogues. Through the cantor you can see who the mem-
bers of his congregation are, the people he represents when
he prays to the Almighty.

As Walt Whitman wrote, great poets need great audiences — without the mass of people great writers are not great, just as the Rabbi in his synagogue is no Rabbi without membership. Therefore, Yiddish literature always concerned itself with "Folk Gantzkeit" — the unity of our people. The rich, the Gedolim like the Kol Hanaorim, the masses, are all part of Yiddish's colorful dimensions. Yiddish and Yiddish literatures have the powers of consolation in times of misfortune — Yiddish literature is as inspiring and demanding as our Torah and Siddur prayers. It strengthens our willpower to remain truthful to our heritage and traditions, and it has kept alive our dreams of the coming of the redeemer. Dispersed among many nations, the whole world became a territory of Yiddish.

From the very beginning in 1507 with the "Bove Bokh" by Eliyahu Bokher, to Leivick and Chaim Grade, despite the cataclysm of the Shoah (the Holocaust), Yiddish literature is alive, is all-worldly, all-Jewish, all-timely. If we consider Mendele the Zeide, or grandfather, of Yiddish literature, the grandmother was an unlikely woman, Glueckel of Hameln, born in Hamburg in 1645.

Daughter of a prominent, patrician family, at the age of 14, she married Hayim Glueckel of Hameln; Hameln was a town near Hanover, Germany, where Jews lived, on and off, since 1277. She raised a family of 12 children in Hamburg, Germany and was her husband's advisor in all business matters. When her husband passed away in 1689, she was able to continue his financial business. Eleven years after Hayim's passing, she married the banker Cerf Levy of Metz. She began to write at the age of 46, "in order to dispel the melancholy" that overcame her after the death of her first husband, and to acquaint her children and grandchildren with their family background. She completed writing the first five sec-

78

tions of her memoirs by 1699. Then, after a pause of 16 years, she resumed her writing and completed two last sections in 1719. Her original manuscript is lost, though copies made by her descendants were preserved.

In 1896 David Kaufmann, an Austrian Jewish scholar and researcher, published her *Memoirs* for the first time, in the original Yiddish, with a lengthy German introduction. Since then, the memoirs have been translated into numerous languages. The memoirs unfold a rich panorama of Jewish life in cities such as Hamburg, Altona, Hameln, Hanover, Metz, Berlin and Amsterdam. They are a source for central European Jewish history and culture and a treasury for those who study linguistics and older aspects of Yiddish language.

Glueckel possessed an excellent memory, a kind temperament and a poetic gift of expression. Her upbringing and a good traditional education gave her a pious disposition. She was well versed in Midrash, in legendary lore and in Talmud, and had read the popular Yiddish ethical books. She often made use of parables, fables, folk maises and stories that illustrate a moral. Here is Glueckel's relating a tale that may be one of the common moral tales that both entertained and instructed:

A philosopher was once walking along the street and meeting an old friend, asked him how things were going. Thanking him, the friend replied: "Badly. No one in the world has more sorrows and troubles than I." Whereupon the philosopher said: "Good friend, come with me to my roof-top. I will point you to every house in the whole city, and tell you the misfortunes and miseries they one and all conceal. Then, if you will, you may cast your own sorrow in with the rest and draw out any other you choose in its stead. Perhaps you will find one more

79

to your liking." Together they climbed to the roof, and the philosopher showed his friend the unhappiness that darkened one house after the other. And he said: "Do now as I told you." But the friend replied: "In truth, I see that every house hides as much woe and hardship as my own, and perhaps more. I think I'll keep what I have."

"Die ganza Welt ist voll Pein,
Ein jeder find't das Sein."
(The world is one long groan,
Which each man calls his own.")

Glueckel was profoundly influenced by Tkhines, devotional Yiddish prayers for women, and often used them in her meditations.

It is amazing that the most precious monument, the "best expression of a woman's role in Yiddish literature" as we recognize Hameln's memoirs did not reach Yiddish readers until nearly 250 years after they were written. Niger writes in *Die Yiddishe Literatur un Die Lezern*, "We do not possess in our literature another book that has such a great cultural-historical value as the memoirs of Glueckel of Hameln." Historians of literature have compared her with the French writer Madame de Sevigné, the great and famous epistolographic genius of letter writing. Szymon Dubnow in the *Welt-Geschichte Fun Yiddishn Folk* writes, "We learned from her memoirs how children were raised, how they were married, how they struggled to survive in a world of anti-Jewish restrictions."

Glueckel was a deeply religious person. Even when she lost one child and then a second child and lived in poverty and had to move into a shack, she accepted her lot and destiny and continued her struggle for survival. In her writings is the history of her generation of Jews — the immigration and emigration of Jewish communities, echoes of the Bogdan Chmielnitzki Pogroms, the movements of false Messiah's, the Shabatai Tzvi followers. Her history is ours.

ABRAHAM SUTZKEVER
Born 1913, Smorgan, near Vilna, Lithuania
He lives now in Tel Aviv, Israel

> *No sad songs please:*
> *Sad songs just tease*
> *At sorrow.*
> *Words, too, betray.*
> *And names, forever,*
> *And tomorow.*
>   A. *Sutzkever*

Poetry is work, time, it is labor, it comes with a mixture of pain and joy. Writing a poem is splitting hard rock with an instrument we call the pen, the sparks of fire are the inspiration that helps form the poem. Poetry is part of creation, an inner power that plays with words, thoughts that develop inside your soul. When the poem is ready and you think that your creation is completed, you may discover that it needs more shaping, more corrections and fine adjustments to seethat body and spirit of the poem are in harmony. One of the great poets of our generation whose compositions are marked by beauty of thought, imaginative language, and new, creative words sparkling like precious-cut jewels is Abraham Sutzkever.

For me, Sutzkever is the spark of fire coming out from the rock of darkness that surrounded us during the Holocaust,

83

that illuminated our road through that dark time. Stuzkever's skillfully written poems and stories possess a hypnotic power — they draw us by their passion for nature and mastery of words, by their imagination and unique forms, like a symphony orchestrated assembly of words, rhythm and musical perfection. "Charred Pearls," written in July 1943 in Vilna Ghetto, is an example.

Charred Pearls

My words tremble so violently they moan,
Like broken hands they plead, entreat,
Helplessly hone
Their edges like fangs lusting for meat.

I'm moved no longer by your howls,
Or written word, fanner of the world's fire:
Instead, charred pearls like emptied vowels
Gaze blankly at me from their pyre.

And not even I, dead already to my death,
Can recognize this woman in flame.
Of all her pleasures, body, being, breath,
Charred pearls are left, not even a name.

Translated by Sarah Zweig Betsky

Sutzkever's style, his poetic spirit, developed in his early youth in Vilna — the Jerusalem of Lithuania, where he was a member of the Young Vilna group of poets, the so-called In-Zich group, who followed a form of introverted writing. Sutzkever's unique lyrics are painstakingly polished, constructed with utmost severity. An innovator and virtuoso in the field of Yiddish language, he is recognized in the world of literature as one of the great poets of our century. For more than 40 years, Sutzkever has been editing the prestigious literary quarterly *Di Goldene Keyt*, one of the outstanding Yiddish magazines — each copy is a juicy pomegranate of poems, short stories, essays, chronicles.

Born in Smargon, he fled with his parents to Siberia during World War I. This chapter of his life was the source of many of his poems. In "In Chuter" ("In the Hamlet"), which is part of a large cycle entitled *Siberia*, he writes:

In the quenched corners of the room
The moon breathes its solitary brilliance.
My father's face is white as the moon,
The snow's silence weighs upon his hands.

Returning to Vilna, Sutzkever became a leading member of the literary-artistic group, "young Vilna." Together with Chaim Grade, Leizer Wolf, Elhanan Wogler, Shmerke Kotcherginski and others, he revolted against old established forms and introduced new verse, fascinating new rhythm, diverse, daring views, ideas, exuberant and rich features, yet holding onto the deep-rooted traditions of the Jerusalem of Lithuania. In 1943, Sutzkever escaped from the Vilna ghetto to the partisans and then to Moscow. After the war, he testified at the Nuremberg Trials. He lived for a while in Lodz, in Paris and in 1947 he settled in Tel Aviv.

In 1988 Sutzkever celebrated his 75th birthday. The Jewish world has bestowed many distinguished honors, doctorates and literary awards on Sutzkever — he helpd in the miracle of resurrecting Yiddish in Israel. The muses are still with him. In "Kernels of Wheat" he exclaims:

Like a hen sheltering its chick —
I run with the Jewish word.
Rummaging in every courtyard.
So its spirit won't be extinguished.

I dedicated the following poem to Abraham Sutzkever after
visiting him in The Hemlin House in Tel Aviv, where he
presented me with his book, *Di Feldroyz* (*The Fieldrose*).

Abraham Sutzkever

Creator of compositions:
mystical, romantic, poems
so simple and appealing.
You're always searching,
striving for certainty,
attempting to find new
tones, new words in old
styles, forms of the past.
Your troubled soul, the
sadness of the Holocaust
comes through your poems.
Not only are the writings
exemplary, but your life,
your actions. The dedicaiton
to the memory of our people,
lives in your creations:
Survival, Resistance, Love,
the rediscovery of our past,
continuation of "The Golden
Chain" gives us a sense of
supernatural beauty, soul,

faith in Netzach Yisroel.
While others are preoccupied
with physical survival,
you carry the torch of
remembering our culture
with talent, hope and joy.
You keep Yiddish alive
as a sacred language of
a people of sacred martyrs
and heroes we must never forget.
We bless the hour when
you survived, to guide us . . .

The *Fieldrose*, poems written between 1970 and 1972, with drawings by Sutzkever's friend Marc Chagall, is a beautiful and astonishing book. I must confess that I have tried to translate some of Sutzkever's work. Every time I looked at a final sentence or phrase, his verbal richness, the profusion of suggestive images — I found different nuances in the original. After several versions, I gave up. . . .

I was privileged to chair a literary event in Baltimore for Abraham Sutzkever. He delivered a stirring appeal to the survivors of European Jewry and lovers of Yiddish that the "one thousand years of history and culture of European Jewry and other communities of Jewish dispersion shall not be forgotten." Years later Chaim Grade, after a lecture and reception in the B'rith Sholom Center in Baltimore, spent several hours with us in a local restaurant. Fortunately, I took notes of that session, which went past midnight:

"I am older than Sutzkever," Grade told us. "Our backgrounds differ, though we have a lot in common: the poverty in which we grew up, the struggle to keep alive.

Our families were crushed by the Nazis and our deep, strong love for the Yiddish language."

Sutzkever was a unique character, different than many of us in "Young Vilna." He was in love with nature, always searching in his nature poems the source of creation. In the depressing reality we all lived in in Vilna, Sutzkever escaped to writing about nature and searching for treasures of Yiddish at the "Yivo."

Sutzkever's poems are an interaction of old Yiddish words with new consonants, new meaning. Everything we loved was decimated by the Nazis; it was detrimental to many of us, but not to Sutzkever. He survived the bloody test of pain and suffering and saved his creative powers. With Sutzkever another miracle happened: His poetic works were saved under the ruins of the Ghetto."

I shared with Grade the deep impression that Sutzkever's poems made on American born students in a Yiddish class at the University of Maryland, the poems, "The Teacher Mira," where Sutzekever tells the story of how the Nazis are daily taking away a number of children from the Ghetto school, but the teacher Mira continues to teach the remaining children.

Chaim Grade became emotional; he started reciting to us from a poem by Sutzkever, "Strashun Street 12" which describes a group of Jews hiding in a cellar, while above on the street the Nazis conduct a Ghetto liquidation action.

"Even when hiding in a wooden coffin, Sutzkever imagines that he is swinging on a boat carried by the waves. This is the secret of his survival." Here is Sutzkever's message to us:

> Survivors! Inherit, with your happiness,
> The tears of each of us, flickering in that vise.
> Remember: Inhale our dying.
> Never forget: Be martyrs to life.

VASSILY GROSSMAN
(Soviet Jewish and Yiddish Writers)
December 12, 1905-September 14, 1964

From Bialik to Joseph Brodsky, from Boris Pasternak to Vassily Grossman, from Isaac Babel to Osip Mandelstam, Russian Jewish writers have been unique talents. Except for Brodsky, each of these writers is dead, though the books by Ilya Erenburg, by Grossman, by Pasternak are now more popular than ever.

Bialik the great Yiddish and Hebrew poet of the 20th century, a genius of extraordinary nature, was lucky to leave the Soviet Union, thanks to the intercession of the Russian novelist Maxim Gorki. Bialik settled in Tel Aviv to a new life in freedom, devoting himself to editing and publishing Hebrew classics. He passed away peacefully on July 4, 1934.

The others were not so lucky. Especially the writers who created in Yiddish. David Bergelson, Der Nister, Dovid Hofshteyn, Samuel Persow, Leib Kwitko, Peretz Markish, Itzik Feffer and others were murdered by Stalin on August 12, 1952 at the Lubianka prison and in other jails in the Soviet Union. There is no parallel in the history of literature of the sufferings and intimidations endured by the Yiddish writers during the Stalin era. The disappearance of Moshe Kulbak and Izi Charick, the arrest and murder of Zelig Akselrod in the summer of 1941, and the Stalin inquisition and execution of the Yiddish writers, artists, scholars in August 1952. Even after Stalin's death, the few writers who survived the gulags and returned to their homes were never publicly rehabilitated and died in obscurity. But their literary legacy survived. Their stories and poems rank among the great works in Yiddish literature. The themes of this literature are characterized by social pathos, struggle for social justice, revolution, the shtetl, the search for a new, better world.

The Party control over Soviet writers in general and Jewish writers in particular was such that every essay, story, poem and novel was analyzed, censored and influenced by so-called literary advisers. Even a writer like Vassily Grossman — author of *Forever Flowing* and *Life and Fate* — called a Soviet Tolstoy, even he, one of the most significant Russian novelists of the 20th century had to submit to the dictates of party consciousness.

Grossman, like some of the other Jewish writers, spent the war years at the front. He was always in the thick of the battle, in the most decisive and dangerous defensive positions or in the first line of attack. He marched and rode from Gomel to Stalingrad and from Stalingrad to Berlin. Vassily Grossman saw everything — the shame, despair, the horror of defeat. Death, ruins, incredible brutality and finally the rapture of victory. He was, along with Ilya Ehrenburg, the most famous and best loved journalist of the war years. But Stalin and his advisers did not trust him. Stalin's commissar of culture accused him of propounding an idealist philosophy hostile to Marxism-Leninism.

Mikhail Sholokhov refused to support the publication of Grossman's novel saying, "Look whom you've allowed to write about Stalingrad. A Jew has no right to depict and glorify the victory of the Russian people." It took Grossman ten years to write *Life and Fate*. When he finished the novel at the beginning of 1960, he reread the enormous 900-page manuscript and sent it to the journal *Znamya*. In February 1961, two KGB agents came to Grossman and searched his room, took the hand-written manuscript, all notes, charts and drafts and left. Grossman wrote to Markov, the head of the Writer's Union; he wrote to Khrushchev, went to Mikhail Suslov, the main party ideologue. Suslov advised Grossman to forget about the novel: "We will publish it in 250 years from now, not before." The book was published in Western Europe, the United States and translated into seven languages.

I elaborate particularly on Vassily Grossman to familiarize you with the severe limitations under which Jewish writers functioned in the Soviet Union. The poet Aaron Kushnirov describes the fate of Yiddish writers in "Hazkarah": "In Neshome, a mayzele shkrapet/ tzi tates, tzi zaydes a nigun,/ nor di tir fun mayn eygenem Shabes/ hot woch mit a shtern farriglt." ("A little mouse grinds my soul/ with my father's or grandfather's melody/ yet the door of my own Shabbat/ was bolted by a guard with a star . . .")

Many of the Soviet Yiddish writers sincerely believed that the Soviet Union offered new hope for humanity and a new future for Yiddish culture. Leib Kvitko and Der Nister returned from Hamburg, Germany, Dovid Hofshteyn returned from Eretz Yisroel, Peretz Markish came back from France and Poland, David Bergelson returned from Berlin and Moshe Kulbak came to Minsk from Vilna. The honeymoon lasted for several years. Yiddish books and literary magazines were published in Kiev, Charkov, Moscow, Minsk. The Yiddish writers were so dedicated to the Soviet system that any word of criticism of the Soviet Union was attacked as "fascistic-capitalistic propaganda."

Beginning in 1929, a new wave of Socialist realism began to dominate the "Yevsection" of the Soviet Union. Kvitko and Hofshteyn were attacked for being too nationalistic in their writing. Writers were arrested, sent to the Gulags or just removed from their positions in the editorial offices of the still-existing magazines.

Word War II mobilized all Yiddish writers for the war to save the Russian motherland. They forgot all the indignities they experienced from Stalin and the Party and dedicated their talents and lives to winning the war against the Germans.

But as soon as the war was over, Stalin started the spiritual and physical liquidation of Yiddish culture and literature. He revived the Blood Libel Trials of the Beilis case of 1911-1913 with a new trial of Jewish doctors, accused of planning to murder all Soviet leaders. He killed Solomon Mikhoels, the director of the Jewish State Theater in Moscow, closed the theater, the publishing house Emes. He arrested and killed the Yiddish writers. Stalin planned to deport all Russian Jews to Siberia. Only the Malach Hamoves, the Angel of Death, in 1953 halted his wicked plan.

Yiddish literature survived Stalin. There existed recently a Yiddish magazine in Moscow: *Sovietish Heimland* where a young generation of Yiddish writers publish their works. Under Perestroika and Glasnost, books by the murdered Yiddish writers were being translated and published in the Soviet Union. In Birobidjan a Yiddish newspaper *Birobidjaner Shtern* continues to be published.

Is there a future for Yiddish literature in the Soviet Union? The answer is no. Anti-Semitism continued after Stalin, after Khrushchev, after Breszhnev and is stronger than ever now. Newspapers, magazines, flyers appear daily, spreading vicious hate against Jews, calling for pogroms. Jews are running from Tbilisi, capital of Georgia, from Leningrad, from towns and cities in Byelorussia and Ukraine. In 1990, 250,000 Jews left Soviet soil.

All the talk about a cultural revival of Judaism and Yiddish culture is not true. The club in Moscow is just a Potiemkin Village used for propaganda. The only place for Yiddish writers to continue writing is in the free world, in America and in Israel. One of the poets who left the Soviet Union in the 1970s was Joseph Kerler. He survived the Vorkuta Slave Labor Coal mines and returned to Moscow but was blacklisted as a nationalist with no opportunity to publish. He visited Washington on several occasions and spoke on behalf of Soviet Jewry. Here are excerpts from a letter he wrote to a fellow Jewish refusnik in the Soviet Union, Nechama Lifshitz, a famous Yiddish folk singer, who has lived in Israel since 1969.

> Dear land where I was cradled!
> I leave you now, not like a beaten dog
> who, at a whistle or a pat, is
> pathetically ready to bound back
> and wag his tail. . .
> I go with a heavy heart,
> with leaden steps, with each step
> I tear away pieces of earth
> soaked with my blood.
> I wrench my eyes away
> I wrench my heart away
> and wish you: Let all be well with you.

All Jewish writers, Jewish leaders, scientists and artists who for years came out of what has been the Soviet Union have one thing in common: a Jewish consciousness. Some were fully assimilated, some had distanced themselves from their Jewish heritage, some were Jewish by birth only, some even expressed hostility toward their own people. Some left Russia to become world Jewish leaders: Chaim Weizman, Elie Metchnikoff, Anton Rubinstein, Marc Chagall, Mendele, Sholom Aleichem, Leivick, Vladimir Jabotinski, A.D. Gordon, Usishkin, Ben Zvi and Zalman Shneur Shazar.

Some decided to stay and participate in the revolution, fighting on the side of the Red Army against the White Army and the Petlyura band who organized pogroms on Jews. Yona Yakir, a former yeshiva student, commanded the 45th Division of the Red Army, defeated the White Army and received the highest military honors.

He later became Commander of the Russian War Academy but Stalin murdered him during the purge of 1937. Bialik's brother-in-law General Y.B. Gamarnik, chief political Commissar of the Russian Armed Forces, committed suicide while Yakir was brought to trial. Other Jews who were active in the leadership of the Soviet Union were Yakov Sverdlow, Trotsky, Litvinov, Volodarski, Uritski, Kaganowitz, scientist Lev Landau, Abram Yoffe, Lina Stern, Yaroslavski and thousands of others. Most of them were arrested and liquidated, as were the Yiddish writers, artists and actors.

Many authors who were fully assimilated, untouched by Stalin, came back to Judaism after the Holocaust and after the establishment of the State of Israel. Just as my Lodz landsman Polish poet Julian Tuwim wrote, "We the Jews of Poland," so did Russian writer Vassily Grossman, a Jew by birth, return to his people and begin to write about the Holocaust, about the murder of the Jews of Berditchev, about the extermination camps, Treblinka and Majdanek. In his epic *Life and Fate* he writes of Jewish suffering, anti-Semitism and martyrdom. Grossman was transformed and felt the pain of his brethren in his own homeland.

Stories and Memoirs

❖ ❖ ❖

LEYBELE

In the city of Lodz, Poland, at #21 Polnocna Street, there was a Gur hasidim shteebl, a prayer and study house where young men devoted their days to Torah and Talmud study. One of these young men known as Leybele was the son of a poor tailor on Wolborska Street. His family moved from Kielce to Lodz in 1929. His father was a simple, humble man who worked hard six days a week trying to support his family. But the oldest son, Leybele, had a keen mind and an urge to study. Although his father prayed in the old community synagogue on Wolborska Street, Leybele was drawn to the Gur hasidim. After completion of the Machzikey Hadas Yeshiva, he began his daily studies at the Gur shteebl.

Leybele was a gifted student and received respectful attention from the other students. He was a nicely groomed young man, tall, with glowing black eyes, curly side-locks and a noble, soft face. But Leybele had one failing. He immersed himself with a religious enthusiasm in studying stories about other worlds. He displayed such a lofty faith in heaven and hell that he constantly spoke of the pain, sufferings, troubles, even the nooks and crannies which are prepared for the deceased. He knew the nature and accompanying punishment of each sin. Because of his constant immersion in the stories of hell, Leybele became imbued with an idea: to suffer the pangs of hell here on earth. The agonizing tribulations the human soul would pass before reaching the Garden of Eden must be dealt with while we are still in this world. As Rabbi Eliezer ben Yaakov said, "As long as a man has peace here on earth, his sins are not forgiven." And Leybele had sinned much. He could not forget the fervent joy spreading through his body when he had the honor to greet the admired Rabbi of Gur, the tsadik Reb Mordecai Alter, on his visit to Lodz. He could not forget the pleasure of a hot plate of borscht served to him by his mother after a long winter fast day on the tenth of Tevet. "A Jew," Leybele preached, "may not derive any pleasures from this world; only spiritual and ethereal thoughts must fill our daily lives."

Aside from this peculiarity, Leybele was a normal yeshiva bachur, a quiet, sincere, and gifted yeshiva student, studying with enthusiasm with other young men at the shteebl on Polnocna Street. The only outward difference between the other students and Leybele was his odd dress, his hungered countenance. Some rabbis attempted to get Leybele to accept decent clothes, to convince him that fasting Mondays and Thursdays was a transgression that violated Jewish laws, endangering his health. They tried to invite him to a Shabbat meal and enjoy the pleasures of the holy day. Leybele always had his answer ready. "I don't care about earthly pleasures. I want to reach our Creator having attained the highest faith, the spark of divine closeness by withdrawing from earthly pleasures, not for the fear of hell but for the pure love of my fellow human beings who are created in G-d's image."

Sad and sordid events arrived. On September 1, 1939, the German armies attacked Poland. The worst nightmare in Jewish history started for Polish Jewry — dark days of humiliation, forced labor for men and women, daily attacks on Jews by the Germans and their Polish hirelings. Some Poles eagerly participated in attacking the students at the shteebl on Polnocna Street. Torah scrolls and holy books were destroyed. Students were taken to the yard of the Pozanski Hospital, herded into a small field, and held there for three days on water only. The Germans did not allow any food brought to them from the hospital for the "enemies of the Reich." Leybele felt that at last the time had come for his ideas to be put into effect. He walked around among the beaten and tormented Jews in the yard, gave them water, washed their wounds, and kept saying, "We must not fear or show weakness. We must show them that we are strong against all forces of darkness."

Leybele's family decided to escape to the Soviet Union. Leybele refused to join them. "Russia is a godless country, religion is considered a crime and is punished with prison terms in Butyrka." He found work in a bakery and remained in Lodz. When the Lodz ghetto was formed and an order was issued by Chaim Rumkowski, the ghetto leader, that "700 Jews must volunteer for work," Leybele was one of the first "volunteers" in line. He was sent to Poznan with a transport of others. In the camp at the Poznan stadium, 1,100 Jews from Lodz and Ozorkow were kept busy building water canals and new roads. Twelve hours daily, in the biting frost of subzero temperatures, they marched ten miles away from their barracks to the road. They were ordered to build with excessive speed, they suffered constant brutal emotional and physical battering. They worked digging loam from the frozen ground, drove hand lorries with sand, cement, stones and loam, received beatings, lashings, had their hands frozen and ribs smashed.

Many collapsed at work, many were shot, others became sick and were executed by the guards. Only one among them did not complain and continued working; that was Leybele. Many of his fellow prisoners took advantage of his good heart and used him. The Germans and the Polish guards made fun of him, had him dance, jump, and make himself act crazy. His face would contort into a pained grimace; only his eyes would reflect a wild glow. "It hurts my dear brothers, but it is good for me. This suffering and humiliation does not compare to the true Gehenom, the true hell. A person must cleanse his body and be prepared for the worst, remembering, I have set the Lord always before me." The starved victims looked with sadness at this thin, pale Leybele with his large, black burning eyes. Pityingly, they shook their head and said, "Poor Leybele, he's just plain crazy."

Leybele's work was to keep the coals burning and spread them on the frozen ground. All other Jews who, together with Leybele, had dragged around the iron bucket filled with burning coals became sick and burned their hands. Leybele remained unharmed, his face became red from fire, but the frosty winds nullified any benefits the coal might have afforded his body. He used to stay by the glow of the burning coals and recite by memory from the Talmud, using the special niggun he used to chant at the Gur shteebl.

"There are five types of fire in hell: Fire which eats, fire which drinks, fire which eats and drinks, fire which neither eats nor drinks, and fire which burns fire. There are mountains of burning coal, lakes of pitch and sulfur which seethe and boil. When a man is brought to hell, satanic devils come and push into the hell fire, and the flames envelope him. How can the burning of one finger compare to the real, great fire of hell? If I could go through all this and sing praises to my Creator, that would be my greatest victory."

When the work at the Poznan stadium was finished, of

the original 1,100 Jews, less than 100 remained. The German camp supervisors ordered a selection. Many of the remaining Jews were in a dreadful condition from the meager food supply, the torture, the agonizing work pace, the daily marches, and the beatings by the guards using whips, pistols, and rifles. This made them unfit for conscription to a new labor column. Only 26 were chosen to be transported to Auschwitz. Leybele was among them. In Auschwitz, Leybele worked in the Pritshenbau Kommando, a carpentry unit which repaired furniture in the Gestapo barracks and built bunks, tiers, windows and doors for the Buna camp. He suffered continually from hunger, he carried a heavy tool box on his shoulder for his foreman, and unloaded huge metal doors used for construction of furnaces. People around him died daily from disease, hunger and beatings. Some were taken for medical experiments, but not Leybele. His legs were swollen. Some fellow prisoners pitied him and gave him bread crumbs. He gave the bread crumbs to half-dead inmates, helpless victims waiting for the next march to the crematoria. Leybele would preach to them.

"There are seven divisions in hell. In each division there are seven thousand houses. In each house there are six thousand windows. In each window there are six thousand vials of gall. Well, what is my running from barrack to barrack compared to the constant driving, running and chasing through seven thousand houses in the other world."

When the daily selections began, when the Buna blocks became abnormally crowded, and the annihilation squads marched more and more people to the gas chambers, when the gallows in Auschwitz multiplied and daily hanging of Jews continued, Leybele began to speak to the inmates with the voice of a prophet.

"Dear brothers, soon we will experience the highest form of torture. We must see that our pain will not be in vain. Let us repent, strengthen our faith, conquer our fears. We will face the Holy Throne as liberated men, free from all pain. You, my dear brothers, have experienced the sufferings mentioned in the Talmud and our holy books. Let us go with joy through the last tortures and we will all be delivered from the gates of hell, cleansed of all sin, free from all sufferings. Let us stand pure before the Heavenly Tribunal."

The people yelled, "Crazy Leybele! Go away and leave us alone. Shut up. The Kapo will get you!" "If he would only get me, then I would know that I was victorious," Leybele said.

Time passed. Leybele turned into a skeleton. He could hardly drag himself around on his thin feet. Now, his new assignment was to remove excrement from the latrine to the fields. Leybele was sad. He feared he would expire with an easy death and that he would not achieve his dream of reaching the highest degree of torture and suffering. His only comfort was that his Creator knew all his thoughts and knew how great Leybele's love and trust in Him was. However, he wanted to make the name of the Almighty accepted by the persecuted, abandoned Jews. He saw how Jews were hung by their feet, how naked people were made to stand for hours in the frost at the place of appeal, how people were beaten and murdered without cause. Their sufferings were greater than his own. He knew why he was suffering, but did they? He envied them.

One morning, during a selection, a father and son in his barracks were separated. The father was taken to work, the boy was condemned as unfit, useless. The father wanted to save his son, even at the cost of his own life. But the barracks where the condemned were held were heavily guarded. Only

Leybele, with his refuse cart, could move freely amidst the barracks. The father attempted to convince Leybele to smuggle him into the barracks in his refuse wagon to free his son. Leybele did not like this plan because it was too risky. He worked out his own plan. He took the refuse wagon and drove it into the yard of the special block area. He called to the boy to quickly change into his stinking clothes and take the wagon out in his place. The boy went out safely with the wagon and Leybele remained inside. The next morning, when the arbeitsunfahige — the group unfit for work — was led to the gas chambers, among the cries of the condemned a joyous voice was heard.

"Ashrecha, Leybele — you are blessed, Leybele — who has merited this occasion. I have conquered fear! I have been victorious against hell."

"Adonai Melech. Adonai Moloch! Adonai Yimloch Le'Olam Voed! God is King. God will be King for Ever and Ever."

KOL NIDRE 1939

In Lodz, Poland, there stood a huge synagogue on Wolborska Street. We all called it the "old city synagogue." When the Sabbath came and Cantor Solovychik prayed with his choir, the synagogue was habitually overcrowded with worshipers. When holidays like Rosh Hashonah and Yom Kippur came, not only was the synagogue filled to capacity but masses of people stood around in the streets wearing their talleism, their religious apparel and listening to the prayers and songs of the cantor.

Every year, on the eve of Yom Kippur, the heavy golden gates of the holy ark were opened. The beautiful crystal chandeliers glistened in the light and shone as if they had been dipped in a magic solution. An elaborate white drape embroidered in gold and silver covered the Holy Ark. Everything seemed to have the holiday glow. When the cantor and the choir would sing, the entire synagogue was filled with such a stillness that one could hear the elderly rabbi sigh at intervals.

My greatest pleasure was just to sit and stare unendingly at the richness and beauty of the surroundings. And so it was this way each year, until 1939 when the war began.

The Germans occupied Lodz just a few days before the holiday. Their first order was that Jews were forbidden to come and pray collectively with the minyan. In the lobby of the "old city synagogue" the German quartered a cavalry squadron. The eve of Rosh Hashoneh, Chaim Rumkovsky, whom the Germans made the leaders of the Jews of Lodz, visited the Jewish vicinities in his carriage. He ordered the Jewish population not to pray collectively, since the Germans issued a warning that those who were caught would be prosecuted.

On Rosh Hashonah, my Uncle Moshe and grandfather, Reb Gershon, although cautioned along with the rest, secretly left our house to visit the home of a rabbi, where they prayed together. Those who were unfortunately caught by the Germans were driven away and never returned. Since this was the situation on Rosh Hashonah, we decided to spend Yom Kippur at home.

On the eve of Yom Kippur, my aunt closed the shutters, locked the doors, covered the table with a white cloth, and commenced to light her candles. My uncle was sitting nearby selecting the holiday prayerbooks. My grandfather was sitting in the corner of a rear room dressed in a long white robe, and wearing his tallis. He sighed heavily and repeated something from his prayer book.

My aunt, cousins and I took the prayer books and tried to read. But our lips felt as though they were fastened together. Something inside gave us the feeling that the holiday prayers were not welcome. We felt as though we were disgraced and forgotten by God.

Suddenly, a bell sounded. The janitor shouted, "Who's there?" extra loud so that we would all be sure to hear it. (That was how we decided for him to let us know if someone was coming.)

"Open! Soldiers."

We quickly blew out the candles while my uncle was hiding the candlesticks, the tallis and the prayer books. Suddenly we heard a riot in the corridor of our home. There was crying and screaming. Two soldiers rushed in.

"All men out to work. Hurry! Hurry! Take pails and washcloth. Hurry! Hurry!"

One German took my uncle and the other dragged out my grandfather, who was trembling with fright. I pleaded, "Please leave the old man, he is sickly. Take me in his place."

Hurriedly he let go of my grandfather and gave me a quick shove. "Hurry out." Out in the street the Germans had lost no time in lining up all our neighbors; men both young and old, together with some women, all supplied with brooms, pails, washcloths and brushes.

They drove us out into the street and placed us among the other Jews from our neighborhood. Many were wearing their long black holiday cloaks. Between the lines with the rest of us stood Rabbi Abraham with his two sons and son-in-law. Frightened and feeble with age, he was aided by his two sons.

It was getting dark. Everyone on Jacoba and Wolborska streets had already bolted their doors. All was quiet: the streets were deserted except for a few German guards who were parading back and forth with machine guns. They drove us into the corridor of the synagogue where the Germans divided us up into groups. I was told to turn the water pump with another man. Some of the men carried water while others groomed the horses and carried away dirt and sand which was replaced with fresh hay.

Rabbi Abraham and his sons worked steadily with iron brushes, combing the horses' bodies. A German soldier, laughing heartily, soon came over and pulled hard at Rabbi Abraham's long grey beard.

"Hey, Jew. Today is your holiday: sing something. But keep working, too." Rabbi Abraham, biting hard to keep angry words back, just kept working with the little strength he had. One of his sons who couldn't stand the manner in which his poor father was being tormented, pleaded with the German guard.

"Please, guard, leave the old man alone. He's working the best he can. Have a little sympathy."

"Keep quiet, you dirty Jew," replied the guard. "Sing I command you." The German then lifted his whip and slashed Rabbi Abraham's feet. The old man, who had been standing with his eyes closed, lifted them to heaven and exclaimed, "Ri-bon-eh-shel-olem." (God in heaven) "Oyb Dir is Lieb — is mir nicho." (It is your desire — it is my pleasure). And he started to sing Kol Nidre.

Rabbi Abraham rubbed hard as he combed the horses' bodies with a rhythmic touch to the melody of his song. With each note the tears fell drop by drop on his long grey beard.

"Louder, Jew!" shouted the guard as he burst out into laughter. "Everyone join in."

I was still turning the handle of the water pump while others were carrying the pails of water and transferring the hay. But everyone kept on singing as they were told to do. The entire corridor of the synagogue was soon full of the Kil Nidre prayer — De-in-dar-noh.

The soldier feared the loud tones and sad melodies. He did not want the officer in the synagogue to hear the songs and so he shouted:

"Stop singing! Enough of that meowing!"

Everyone stopped almost instantly, with the exception of Rabbi Abraham. He kept singing on as though he had not heard the soldier. With an entranced expression on his wan face, and his eyes full of fire, his shattered voice sang on "M'yom Kepurem Zeh" (From this Yom Kippur on).

Rabbi Abraham failed to obey the soldier's orders and so he was whipped and slapped about his face and body. The old man turned about and fell. The soldier again picked up the whip to strike him again, but Rabbi Abraham's son sprang forth, much to the soldier's amazement, and grabbed at his wrist to hold him back.

"Soldier, this is my father. He is 76 years old. If you insist on whipping someone, whip me."

The soldier started to reach for his revolver, but fortunately the officer emerged from the corridor of the synagogue. The chores had been completed, and everyone was told to get back in line and march onward home. The old Rabbi Abraham, still lying on the ground and hardly able to walk, was assisted to his feet. His bloody face was washed with cold water to revive him, and he was taken under his arms and placed in line with the others.

All was quiet on the way home. Bitten lips were tightly shut from shame and fear. Rabbi Abraham who was mumbling to himself glanced up to heaven and replied in very short words, "Al daath hakohol."

Suddenly he looked around himself and called out: "Well, Jews, why are you all keeping silent? Sing further Kol Nidre!"

PURIM 1940:
A Defiant Rabbi Thwarts the Nazis

The town of Lask in the Lodz province, central Poland, had a Jewish community for 300 years. Jews were engaged in trade, crafts, business, supported their own communal organizations, had their own rabbi since 1726 (Reb Israel B. Ithamar), and their own representatives in the municipal Council. Lask had two libraries, chedorim (Hebrew elementary school), Tarbut Hebrew school, a Beth Yaakov School for girls, and "Maccabi" and "Shtern" sports clubs. Despite threats against the Jewish community by anti-Semites, and high taxes levied against Jewish businessmen, the Jews of Lask led a spiritually rich Jewish life.

At the outbreak of World War II, there were 3,864 Jews in Lask. The leader of the religious community was Yehuda Leib Aizenberg, a rabbi, a genius and noted scholar, respected by the Chasidim and modern, progressive Jews. His brilliance was known all over the Jewish world and his family had a history of 55 generations of rabbis. It often happened that great rabbis occupied rabbinical posts in small cities and towns. Such was the situation with Rabbi Aizenberg, the rabbi of Lask, who perished by the hands of the Nazis. His death was one of the most bizarre of the Nazi murders during the Holocaust.

His long martyrdom began with the Nazis' arrival in Poland. The Nazis used all madness, pain, mockery, ridicule and diabolical wit to inflict pain on this unusual Jew. But this great spirit of a man knew how to overcome all the temptations and pains. He reached a holiness that many could never comprehend. The first trial came in 1940 before the first Purim of the German occupation.

The Nazi commandant of the town of Lask came to their rabbi and gave him an order: "Herr Rabiner, we Germans would like to celebrate this year's Purim together with the Jews. But we will celebrate in a German manner. We will erect a Purim gallows and hang Jews. We Germans are compassionate; the Jews hanged Haman's ten sons, we will hang only two Jews. You, rabbi, must choose the two Jews. You will decide who the two Jews are going to be. I am giving you three days. . . ."

The rabbi felt short of breath; after a moment of anxiety, he got his breath back and with a clear voice, said to the Nazi: "I don't need three days. I don't have much to think about or choose. I have the two Jews for you. One is me; the second my wife. Other Jews I will not deliver to you."

The Nazi was astounded by the rabbi's quick and bold answer. He saw in this Jewish impudence and got mad: "How dare you, a Jew, talk to a German officer in such a bold tone? You, Herr Rabiner, I need for other occasions and other purposes. For Purim hangings, I need other Jews and you will deliver them." This is what the Nazi said, leaving the house.

The sad news spread all over town, the Nazi's request and the rabbi's answer. Jews were obsessed by despair. What could they do? Not only were a lament and wailing heard among the Jews; but also a spirit of holiness, of sacrifice, when they learned that their rabbi had offered himself and his wife as

112

martyrs for his community. Jew after Jew came to the rabbi saying, "We would like to sacrifice ourselves for our town, for our Jewish community."

But the rabbi insisted that he would never deliver two Jews to the Nazi Commandant.

❖ ❖ ❖

Purim passed. The commandant was filled with vicious hate against the rabbi who did not fulfill his wish. One day he ordered that all the Jews and the rabbi of Lask be assembled in the Market Place. The whole population was gathered and surrounded by SS troops and guards. From the villages around the town, the Polish population came to look for a spectacle.

On a nod from the Nazi commandant, a priest appeared, holding a cross. He stopped in front of the rabbi who was surrounded by his community. The Nazi commandant walked over to Rabbi Aizenberg and ordered him to bow and kneel before the cross.

All eyes were on the rabbi and the cross before him. The Jews were full of fear, the Christians full of curiosity to see the struggle between the rabbi and the Nazi, the conflict between Jew and Christian. What would happen? Would the rabbi prostrate himself before the cross? What would happen if he refused to kneel? Jews, Christians, the Nazi and his guards, heaven and earth — all waited in silence.

But the silence was interrupted by the sound of a loud slap and another smack. When Rabbi Aizenberg moved from his place, the mass thought that he had decided to touch the cross, but he turned toward the Nazi commandant and slapped his face.

The people were in great shock, as if an earthquake had hit the town. The Nazi commandant, ashamed, surprised, grabbed for his revolver.

"This is what I wanted," the rabbi said loudly. He stood proudly, put his chest forward: "You can shoot me now." The Nazi swallowed his shame. He did not shoot, but ordered the rabbi arrested.

The next day, the population was ordered to assemble in the Market Place. There was a gallows. They led the rabbi to the gallows, and he kept saying his confession before death. They hanged him, but he fell to the ground in pain, with cramps. This was planned by the German doctors and the Nazi commandant: "Hang him but do not kill him."

Half choked, he was released from the rope and taken back to jail where the doctor worked on him. Next morning, he was hanged again, and on the third day, again. After the third hanging, his body hardly moving, he was given to the Jews: "Here is your rabbi — take him away."

The same night, the rabbi was taken to Lodz Ghetto, where they operated on his broken neck bones. It took many weeks until he was able to move his head and walk.

❖ ❖ ❖

As soon as he felt he could walk, he insisted that they help him return to Lask Ghetto, to his community. They begged him to stay in Lodz, but he did not want to give in: "I want to, I must return to my people." And he went back to Lask.

When, in August 1942, the Lask Ghetto was liquidated and of the 3,500 Jews, 800 craftsmen were sent to the Lodz

Ghetto and 2,700 to Chelmno Concentration Camp, Rabbi Yehuda Leib Aizenberg was with them. On the way to Chelmno, he asked the guard for permission to pray. He was weak and fellow Jews supported him on their shoulders. He looked at the prayer book and, pretending to the guards that he was praying, he called to his people to flee. Crying out in a tongue the guards did not understand, he repeated over and over his "prayer."

"There are only so many guards, and you are in the thousands. You know where they are taking us. Dear children, run, save yourselves. They will kill some of you, but not all of you. Save yourself, run. God will protect you."

Those who listened to their rabbi, and ran, lived to tell his story.

MARTYRDOM AND RESISTANCE
April 19, 1943

This is the way it was on April 19, the night of Pesach, 1943, as described by the Yiddish poet Binem Heller:

"Pesach has come to the Ghetto again.
The wine has no grape, the matzoh no grain,
But the people anew sing the wonders of the old.
The flight from the Pharaohs, so often retold.
How ancient the story, how old the refrain!
The windows are shuttered. The doors are concealed.
The Seder goes on. And fiction and fact
Are confused into one. Which is myth? Which is real?
Come all who are hungry! invites the Haggadah.
The helpless, the aged, lie starving in fear.
Come all who are hungry! and children sleep, famished.
Come all who are hungry! and tables are bare."

When we will reach chapter 22 in the Passover Haggadah as we read "Vehe sheomdo — and this promise has been our fathers' support and ours: for not one tyrant only has risen up against us to destroy us, but in every generation tyrants have sought to destroy us, and the Holy one, Blessed is He, has delivered us from their hands."

117

We will set down the wine cup, uncover the Matzoh and tell our children, our families and guest at our Seder the following story:

In a Slavic country in the very heart of Europe, between the Bug and Odna rivers and the Baltic and Tatra mountains, among a population of 30 million Poles, lived a community of over 3 million Jews. For ten centuries the Poles and Jews lived as neighbors, each with their own identity. Together they went through times of prosperity, cultural growth and tragic periods of occupation, wars of independence, revolutions, pogroms and famine, despite religious diversity and cultural and economic differences, leading often to the most tragic outbursts against minorities and Jews. The times of wars, under the motto "for your freedom and ours," Jews served their country, fought for Poland under Berek Yoselewicz in the wars of Poland's liberation, linking their future and their fate with Poland's struggle for freedom.

For four centuries Jews lived in Warsaw, Poland's capital on the Vistula River. In 1939, Warsaw's population numbered 1.2 million; of these, 375,000 were Jews. Side by side with Poland's cultural life, art, music, theater, cinemas, museums, literature, and institutions of higher education, the Jews of Warsaw developed their own culture, libraries, theaters, publishing houses, yeshivot, gymnasiums, Yiddish and Hebrew culture. Warsaw had close to 800 synagogues and six daily Yiddish newspapers. The city was the cultural nerve of Orthodox and modern Judaism in Europe.

By September 1942, over 300,000 Jews were sent by cattle cars to Treblinka. By January 18, 1943, only 50,000 Jews remained in what had become the Warsaw ghetto. From the moment the Germans occupied Warsaw, their aim was to liquidate the Jewish community. Heinrich Himmler decided that on April 19, 1943, he would liquidate the ghetto entirely, as a present to Adolph Hitler, whose birthday was April 20. Himmler's aim was to make Warsaw Judenrein — free of Jews.

"The ghetto was surrounded by special forces of German police, gunners, zappers, 2,000 Waffen SS, and several thousand SS troop volunteers. Some 600 men and women of the Jewish fighting organization (Z.O.B.) were under the command of Mordechai Anielevicz and armed with molotov cocktails, hand-grenades, rifles and pistols. Men, women and some groups of Jewish youngsters attacked the Waffen SS from windows and tunnels. This unexpected, violent attack put the German troops to flight, leaving behind their dead and wounded.

"They rallied, but were again repulsed, and the fighting spread to the north. The Germans brought in tanks. When they first appeared at the corner of Mila Street, they were hit by several well-aimed molotov cocktails and set on fire. The second tank suffered the same fate. Once again the Germans withdrew. The Jewish fighters and non-combatants alike were overjoyed. "Those faces which only yesterday reflected terror and despair," wrote one eye-witness, "now shone with an unusual joy difficult to describe. A joy imbued with the pride that the ghetto was fighting.

"On the German side, Colonel Von Sammern was removed from his command that very morning by Himmler's emissary, the SS General Jurgen Von Stroop, who then took over command of the operation himself. Soon after midday he sent in light artillery in support of troops who had abandoned marching orders and advanced through the streets in single file, hugging the walls. These more military tactics had their desired effect. The Jewish fighters put up a fierce resistance, but their light weapons were no match for an artillery bombardment. Their supplies of grenades and bottles of explosives were running out. They were forced to evacuate the shelled buildings: covering their retreat with the remaining hand-grenades and molotov cocktails, they withdrew deeper into the ghetto, taking their dead and wounded with them. Through the afternoon of April 19, the street fighting swayed to and fro.

"The Jews in one block held out for the rest of the day. They had a heavy machine-gun mounted on the roof and kept the enemy at bay until darkness fell. Stroop withdrew all his men from the ghetto for the night. Anielevich and his staff met and made plans for the following day.

"Early on the morning of April 20, German police surrounded the houses whose defenders had defied all efforts to dislodge them. Two bullet-riddled flags were flying from the rooftops: the red-and-white Polish flag and the white-and-blue Jewish flag. The Germans opened fire on the houses and hurled hand-grenades at the windows, but they were repulsed with machine-guns. After half an hour the Germans brought up four small tanks, and their cannon subjected the houses to a fierce bombardment: the defenders hurled grenades at the tanks but were unable to damage them. By then the houses were very much battered and the defenders were much reduced in able-bodied men and ammunition. The Germans stormed the position and hand-to-hand fighting ensued. One group of Jewish fighters, having run out of ammunition, was taken prisoner. Most of them were wounded later they were all shot on the spot."

In the afternoon, Stroop led 300 SS in an attack on one well-defended area. The Jews there, commanded by Marek

Edelman, had mined the roadway. When the Germans advanced, the mines were set off and more than twenty soldiers were killed.

The ghetto was still holding out on April 21. The German losses, moreover, had been greater than expected. Stroop then gave orders to set the ghetto on fire. This gruesome change in the situation was recorded in a communique from the Jewish fighting organization.

"The fires were started by the demolition and incendiary detachments of the German artillery. Columns of smoke are hanging over the ghetto and are growing larger by the hour. The force with which the fire is raging is indescribably fierce. The ghetto streets are enveloped in a thick, corroding smoke.

"Realizing that in armed combat they will not crush the resistance of the Jewish fighters, the Germans decided to destroy them by fire. Thousands of women and children are being burned alive in these houses . . . people, enveloped in flames leap from the windows like live torches. . . ."

On April 23, Stroop advised his superiors, "the action will be completed this day." He was wrong. On that day, Mordechai Anielevich sent a letter by a woman courier to his liaison officer outside the ghetto walls, telling him of the situation and asking for more weapons:

"What has happened has surpassed our most daring expectations. Twice the Germans fled from the ghetto. . . . I have a feeling that great things are happening, that what we have undertaken is of tremendous significance.

"It is impossible to describe the conditions under which the Jews in the ghetto are living today. Only a few will survive. All others will perish sooner or later. Their fate is sealed. In practically all the bunkers where thousands of Jews are hiding, it is impossible to light a candle for the lack of air!"

"The fighting groups continued to hold out, but they were being driven into an ever-narrowing area: the German superiority in armament and manpower was making the outcome of the struggle obvious, no matter how heroic or desperate the defense of the ghetto. On the night of April 27, after more than a week's fighting, Anielevich and other leaders held a meeting in a bunker at which it was decided to evacuate the ghetto and endeavor to join the partisans in the forests. One of the couriers, Regina Fudin, was given the task of contacting the scattered groups of fighters and arranging their withdrawal. The way out of the ghetto was to be through the sewers, which meant that help would be needed from the Jewish fighting organization's representatives on the other side of the ghetto wall and from members of the Polish Workers Party, a left-wing underground organization.

"The exodus began the following night, April 28, when forty fighters led by Regina Fudin entered the sewers near the headquarters bunker. A most painful moment for them was taking leave of their badly-wounded comrades who could not be moved. It was hoped that most of them would follow later, but the Germans soon discovered the hospital bunker and killed all the wounded, together with the men guarding them."

The party of forty-one emerged from the sewers on the Aryan side during the night of April 29, and were hidden in the attic of a Polish worker until the following night, when members of the left-wing underground movement took them in a truck out of Warsaw and to a forest where a partisan unit received them.

The next attempt by a group of Jewish fighters to escape through the sewers, on the night of April 29, ended in tragedy. The Germans had heard of the previous escape and an armed party was in readiness for the next: when the exhausted

Jews had emerged from the manhole, they were mowed down by concentrated fire.

There were still isolated groups of resistance fighters and non-combatants in the ghetto at the beginning of May. The largest was the bunker which served as the headquarters of the fighting organization. It held some three hundred elderly men, women and children, and about eight fighters commanded by Anielevich: from this bunker he kept in touch with agents outside the ghetto. On May 8, SS troops surrounded the area and the bunker's five entrances, although how the Germans discovered the bunker is not known to this day. The non-combatants gave themselves up, but Anielevich and eight men decided to fight it out. The Germans tossed in hand-grenades and then, when the Jews still refused to surrender, sent in poisonous gas. The men in the bunker either choked to death or committed suicide, all except a handful who were near the exits and collapsed from the gas, but were not fatally affected. They were later discovered by the next party intending to escape through the sewers who helped them to get away.

This party numbered about 50 and was led by Marek Edelmen, who had taken over command of the remaining fighters after Anielevich had met his death in the bunker. On the morning of May 10, the party reached its exit point; for many hours they had been forcing a way through the filthy, stinking waters of the sewers, their weapons tied around their necks and some carrying their gassed comrades on their backs. The manhole was pried open: the Polish left-wing underground had a truck waiting and the escapees were taken to join their comrades of the previous exodus.

However, not all of the fifty or so managed to emerge in time. When thirty-four had been loaded into the truck there was a sudden alert that the Germans were approaching. The truck was driven off and the remaining Jews were left in the sewer to await its return. In the meantime, police and SS troops arrived and prepared an ambush. The Poles tried to get through to warn the men in the sewer but were unsuccessful. When the latter lost patience and started to emerge they found themselves face to face with the enemy. The uneven fight was soon over.

On May 16, General Von Stroop was able to report that "the former Jewish residential district (a German euphemism for ghetto) in Warsaw no longer exists."

Nevertheless, the silence among the charred rubble of the ghetto was broken now — and again as the last of the Jewish fighters, compelled to emerge from hiding places in search of food, shot it out with the Germans. There are eye-witness accounts of clashes between Jews and Germans in June and as late as July. In October 1943, the Germans brought in several hundred Jews from Auschwitz concentration camp to clear up the ghetto debris. A survivor of this slave labor later told of entering a bunker and finding on the table the fresh remains of a meal and open book of short stories in Yiddish.

The last recorded report of a Jewish fighting group wandering through the ruins of the ghetto appeared in a Polish underground publication dated July 1944. According to the publication, in June of that year a Jewish group attacked a detachment of armed police passing the ghetto area and killed three Germans. In the retaliatory action that followed, the Germans rounded up and shot twenty-five Jews. Individuals hiding in ghetto caves survived until the uprising of the home army on August 1, 1944, and most of them fell in the three months of fighting that ensued.

Pesach has come to the ghetto again.
The lore-laden words of the Seder are said,
And the cup of the Prophet Elijah awaits,
But the Angel of Death has intruded instead.
As always — the German snarls his commands.
As always — the words sharpened — up and precise.
As always — the fate of more Jews in his hands;
Who shall live, and who shall die, this Passover night.
But no more will the Jews to the Slaughter be led
The truculent jibes of the Nazis are past.
And the lintels and door posts tonight will be red
With the blood of free Jews who will fight to the last.
Pesach has come to the Ghetto again.
And neighbor to neighbor the battle-pledge gives!
The blood of the German will flow in the Ghetto
So long as one Jew in the Ghetto still lives!
In face of the Nazi — no weeping, no wincing!
Only the hatred, the wild satisfaction
Of standing against him and sadly resisting.
Listen! how Death walks abroad in the fury!
Listen! how bullets lament in their flight!
See how our History writes END to the story.
With death heroic, this Passover night!

The Warsaw Ghetto Uprising inspired the Jewish rem-
nants of Eastern Europe, the Partisans, the inmates of con-
centration camps, Jews serving in the allied forces. The ghetto
fighters' spirit gave vigor to the Hagana and the Irgun, who
resolved to establish a homeland for the remnants of our people
in Eretz Israel.

The American Jewish community through the American

Joint Distribution Committee, Jewish labor committee, and the VAAD Hatzalah turned actively to save those Jews who were left and to help them go to Israel and to countries where they could continue to live in freedom and dignity, and to practice their faith and traditions.

This is the story of the Warsaw Ghetto Uprising we commemorate on the night of Passover. A story of unity forgotten among the remnants of the Warsaw Jews, a story of raised spirit, a story with a battle cry: no submission! a battle for freedom and dignity of human and Jewish honor.

Despite the promises by SS General Jurgen Von Stroop that he would spare all fighters who would surrender, they chose to leap from the burning roofs with the Shema Yisroel on their lips, or to sing ani maamin. . . .

The Warsaw Ghetto martyrs and heroes left us a testament: a determination not to tolerate hate, bigotry and dark forces that are inimical to freedom and dignity; to hold fast to the memory of our people who perished in the Holocaust; and to remember their struggle and martyrdom from generation to generation.

Note: Excerpts here are from Len Ortzen: Famous Stories of the Resistance, St. Martin's Press, 1979.

THE UNFORGETTABLE
Interview with Holocaust survivor N: 61856
(Name withheld upon request)

On March 10, 1945, I was liberated from the Stutthof (Sophienwalde) Concentration Camp. I was no longer katzet inmate No. 61856, but once again my human self, free to think and to do what I wished.

My first longing was to seek out my mother and younger sister. According to the messages I had received about them, they should have been in liberated Torn (Toru'n) in Poland. With a permit that I had obtained from the Russian "Komandantura" (Military Command), I set forth in that direction. While still searching for my loved ones, I heard that my mother had died in the Torn labor camp, and that my little sister, together with other women, had been taken out of the Riga Ghetto, transported to Stutthof and killed upon arrival. I was deeply depressed by this ghastly news.

But where could I go? My home town in Germany, was still in enemy hands. In this condition of despair, while still wearing my prison garb, hungry and freezing, I sat in the railroad station of Schneidermuhl (Pila) and waited for a chance to travel on.

The station had been partly wrecked by bombs and artillery. The few remaining small undamaged halls were filled with Russian and Polish soldiers. I found a dry corner among the ruins of the destroyed buildings, and I curled up and went to sleep.

During my disturbed sleep, I could feel the rain and my soaked shirt clinging to my back. I tried to get up and find a dry spot, but I could not move. My feet refused to support me. With great effort, I managed, at last, to rise from the cold wet stones. I walked a few yards, but I soon fell. Not long after this I again fell asleep.

Still between sleeping and waking, I finally realized that soldiers had run to me and were talking and shouting in a strange language. They lifted and carried me into a room. Drops of valerian in water were poured into my mouth. They rubbed my forehead. They spoke to me, but I could not understand them. I wanted to know what had happened to me, but I could not talk. At this moment, a tall man wearing decorations came into the room. He was an officer, as I could see from the epaulets that he wore. He peered into my eyes, felt my pulse, and ordered everyone out of the room.

"Kto ty jestesz?"

"I do not understand."

The officer bent lower, and I could feel his hot breath on my ear.

"Wer bistu?"

I thought it was all a dream, a sweet dream. Did I hear a Yiddish word spoken? I opened my eyes wide and stared into the officer's face. It was more an exclamation than a question when I said,

"A Jew!"

"Yes, and you?"

"I too. Where am I?"

"You are with a Sanitary Battalion spending the night, by

chance, in Schneidermuhl. What are you doing here? How did you come?"

I told him my story.

"I am travelling in the direction of Stettin. Will you come with us?"

"Yes."

This Jewish Officer was in command of a Sanitary Battalion in the Polish 2nd Army. He took me in as a "nurse." I was given a military coat, a warm padded cap, a pair of Russian boots, and a Red Cross bag containing cotton, wool, iodine, ointment, and a pair of scissors. There I stood — a complete military "Nursing Sister."

On our journey, there were several clashes with as yet unconquered groups of German soldiers. We had to retire to deserted villages, where we would spend a few days doing laundry work, overhauling ambulances, and preparing food. At last, on a gray, rainy day, early in the morning, we reached Deutsch Krone, a little Pomeranian town not far from the former Polish border.

While soldiers prepared houses for our "San-bat," the Captain, a soldier, a Jewish lad from Lodz, and myself went to have a look at the town. The gaping windows of the ruined houses looked like empty eye sockets.

The Captain said, "Stalingrad, Smolensk and Warsaw look the same."

The soldier replied, "The Ghetto in Lodz looks the same way, and blessed be the hands of those who so accurately hit the nests in which the murderers lived."

Inside and around the houses lay bodies of stout Germans, dead dogs, bottles of wine that were never drunk, jars of preserves, cooking-fat, and a plated Russian samovar. The samovar must have been a trophy from 1941. We touched nothing, for we felt a deep disgust for everything present, including the dead householder and his bulldog. We did not come as plunderers who would help themselves to the belongings of those who were dead.

The streets were littered with dirt and bed-feathers. Germans were driving the rubbish carts and German women were sweeping the pavements. After several years of experiences in ghettoes and the concentration camp, and after so long a period of moral humiliation, I looked at the little picture before me with satisfaction. The German women were filling the dirt-carts, cursing the world together with the dictator whose picture was seen in the middle of a poster that one of the women was holding.

The Captain smiled and said to himself, "Justice is a wheel, and that wheel turns!"

Jacob, the young Jew from Lodz was a good fellow. I should not have expected such a wan-looking youth to be so full of energy. In every emergency, he was the first to volunteer. I spoke about him to the Captain and he explained.

"Man is a good-natured animal, you can compare human nature with water. Water tends always to flow downward, but if you boil it, up and up it springs; and if you steam it and force it through pipes, it can rise to a mountain top. Is that its nature? No! An alien power has taken possession of it and made it do these things. It's the same with a man. You can bring him to such a pitch that he will do what is far, far away from being what is natural to him. "

Jacob told me many interesting facts that I did not know. For instance, he told me about the Jewish generals in the Russian Army, the Jewish brigade in the British Army, Majdanek, Babi Yar, Treblinka, the Lodz Ghetto, and Herr

Hans Bibov, the "Reich's Representative" and executioner of Lodz Jewry.

Hans Bibov was the one who "set the water on to boil" and made of a good-natured, generous and lovable youth a man who now lived for one thing only, and that was revenge; revenge to be taken on Hans Bibov. The Lodz youth had never come across Bibov, but he kept looking for him on German soil. He could see Bibov's murderous face in every Nazi that he met. To him, every German village represented Bibov's home. For every German, he had only one greeting, one speech, namely, hate.

❖ ❖ ❖

Melancholy days.

Outside, the rain fell without a break. We were encamped in a village near Zlatow. I was on night-duty in the ambulatorium.

The instruments had been boiled and placed in the sterilizer. I had no more duties to perform, so I sat and made notes in my journal. The Captain sat on his camp bed, read a front line newspaper, and smoked. Jacob came in from his post. His coat was soaked through and through. He grumbled.

"A damned country and a damned climate. It does nothing but pour."

The Captain asked, "Perhaps you would like to warm yourself with a drink?"

"Thanks, Captain, I would like a cup of tea."

I put away my pages and started making tea The Captain and I had become very fond of Jacob. Indeed, his simplicity, honesty, and modest behavior had made him a general favorite among the men. His courage, his promptness, and quickness of mind in any clash had won him the respect and admiration of his fellow soldiers. I had learned, besides all this, that he wrote verses.

The Lodz youth said, "I had never in my life written anything, but lately I felt an inner urge to write." Thus he excused himself for his writing, as any shy child might.

The Captain laid his newspaper aside and turned to him: "While the tea-kettle is boiling, tell us something about yourself and your life. "

The soldier did not need to be asked twice. He pulled off his wet boots, sat down by the stove, took his rifle in his hand, cleaned it bit by bit, and related the following

"My name is Jacob Mandelbaum. I was born in Lodz where I went to Cheder and public school. Later, I became a weaver. I worked and studied, attended classes, borrowed books, made acquaintance with Jewish and general literature, associated with others of my age, and had a good time until 1939."

When the Germans entered Lodz, I escaped to Bialystok. From there I travelled toward Russia. My parents and my younger sister remained in the Lodz Ghetto. Up to 1941, I worked in a coal-seam in the Don Basin, and after that I was in Central Asia on the banks of the Darya. By day, I was scorched by the sun; and by night, I shivered with malaria and the scorpion's bite. My hands were swollen from plucking "Djugara" (barley), "Chlopok" (cotton) and rice. After that, I served in the Soviet Army on the Leningrad front. I received distinction, awards, medals, and a wound. I then returned to the front again, but this time I served in the Polish Army. As a Polish soldier, I took part in the marches from Kiev to Lodz. All this toughened and strengthened me. I had looked death in the face many times, but the longing for home, the love for my parents, my only sister, and the hope of seeing them again, gave me the courage to carry on through every hardship. Five long years I held fast to the hope that I still had a home, and that I still had a little sister, father, and mother.

On January 19, this year, I was among the first with my army unit to break in and take possession of my home-town. The moment I was given a few hours leave, I headed for the Ghetto. Upon arriving there, I realized that I had become an orphan. I stood still and gazed at the narrow street in which I was born and raised. The ruins gazed back at me like tombstones. The wire enclosing the Ghetto twisted itself around my neck like a serpent and choked back my tears. I roamed the once familiar streets looking for a trace of my home life, something that was still mine, the faintest reminder of what had been "I" of the former days; but the work of Bibov's executioners had been done with German precision and thoroughness. The Ghetto had been destroyed and Lodz Jewry had been dispatched to Radogoshtsh, Chelmno, Treblinka and Auschwitz.

With a heart turned to stone, I left what had been my home, and I vowed as I took my last look at the ruined Ghetto, that I would take revenge on the Bibovs, and that I would repay them for the Yellow Badge, and for the "Children Liquidation Campaign. With the shot and shell from the Russian automatic guns, I would repay them with interest."

At this point, his tale came to an end. His weapon, which he was cleaning as he spoke, was now clean and bright. He carefully put it away in a corner as though it were a precious treasure. He then took his filled cup of tea and drank it. After this, he took a faded photograph out of the pocket of his shirt. Attached to the photograph were decorations and medals which were held in a scrap of newspaper. On the photograph was a Jew with a sparse beard and a skull-cap, and beside him was a woman wearing a silken shawl and a "Shield of David" brooch on her breast.

"Sir, Captain, these are my parents," the youth stated.

"He resembles my own father of blessed memory," sighed the Captain.

"And she," I whispered to myself "is like my mother."

Who could have foreseen that this was to be my last talk with Jacob.

We made our way through a wooded district. The main roads were crowded with mechanized armored divisions hurrying day and night in the direction of Berlin. Horse and cart transport had to detour through woods and scattered villages.

Late evening — the rain pelted down monotonously. We were surrounded by woods. The signpost indicated that the next village was three kilometers distant, that is, twenty-one kilometers from Deutsch Krone.

Suddenly there was a hailstorm of shots over our heads.

Jacob jumped down, and was followed by a few more soldiers. They opened fire on the woods, but the shooting went on. Stray bullets hit a comrade here and there, and among those hit was Jacob. In the noise and commotion around us, his last groan was not heard. With all haste, they dug his grave by the roadside. By the light of a flashlight, they wrote on a board:

> JACOB MANDELBAUM-SHEREGOVI (PRIVATE)
> BORN 1922 IN LODZ
> FALLEN — MARCH 20, 1945
> HONOR HIS MEMORY

A few stones were heaped on the grave. For one minute, we stood there taking a silent farewell, and then we moved on.

A young Pole, a trooper from the Lodz district, said to me sadly, "That is the soldier's lot. One moment he is here and the next gone. Today I made up with him to have baked potatoes. Who can tell where anyone of us will be tomorrow?"

We reached the village of Hohenstein in the domain of Georgestal and encamped for a night's rest. We dressed the wounds of the injured. In the morning, the most serious cases would be sent to the hospital in Schneidermuhl or Neugard. The Captain, in a white overall, sat on his bed, and appeared very sad. On a little table before him lay the papers and the medals of Jacob Mandelbaum. In his hand, the Captain held the photograph of the fallen one's father and mother. His eyes were full of tears. He, the man who went through the Kursk offensive, who was in the attack on Warsaw, who had performed many operations, and seen every horror that war brings — this man wore the look of one mourning his own brother or son.

The Captain read the two stanzas of a poem found among the papers; simple, unpublished verses ina soldier's language, but how lucid, how heartfelt, how spontaneous were those unstudied lines! Here are the verses of a poem scribbled with a pencil and entitled, Mein Schwesterl (My Little Sister)

> In a dream, when the moon was bright,
> You came where I lay at rest.
> In your arms you held me tight,
> And you cried with your head on my chest.
> You awakened the days of old,

135

The past that in me was sleeping.
And down your cheeks so cold
The tears were silently creeping.
We two, together we wept
For a grief in the vanished years.
We were mourning our parents' death,
And I woke in tears. . . .

A knock was heard on the door. A Corporal in his 30s entered, saluted, and addressed the doctor.

"Panie Kapitanie, allow me to take down the name of the fallen one!"

"Who are you? Was he known to you? Was he your friend?"

"No. I did not know him personally, but I desire to know who he was, because I also am a Jew."

The Captain handed the Corporal the military booklet of Jacob Mandelbaum. The Corporal then copied the name from the booklet.

From outside, from the woods, came the sound of heavy firing The Corporal asked the Captain, "Allow me to go into the woods and give them more than they are looking for."

"I cannot send you. There are only twenty-six of you, but we have no idea of how many they have in the woods. We expect reinforcements tomorrow. Besides, you are under other orders. I can do nothing without your own commander's approval.

The Corporal replied, "Captain, I have been at the front since 1943. The bullets have hailed down on me many times and my uniform is torn by the splinters of explosives. I want to live. I have a mother in Oktiubinsk, may she have long healthy years. I have relatives in Palestine, and that is where I long to be if I survive this war. While my heart beats, I want to fight; and should I fall, I want to die knowing that the German soldiers I have shot dead will spill no more Jewish blood. Captain, you are a fellow Jew; you cannot help but understand me! I have seen in Lublin-Maidanek the crematorium, the gas-chambers, the heaps of human bones, barrels of human fat, the. . . ."

"Say no more!" The Captain said. "Look here!" He showed the Corporal the photograph of Jacob's parents. "There are the mother and father of the fallen Mandelbaum. It might be a likeness of my own, or of hers (he pointed to me). They perished for no reason except that they were Jews. Go into the woods with your men! In the absence of your commander, you will take his place. Go and God help you!"

Night. My sleep was troubled. I heard the whistling shriek of the grenades, the firing, and the ceaseless roar of the machine-guns. The fight raged throughout the woods. The noise often awakened me, but weariness will have its way, and I fell asleep again, I dreamed of the Stutthof Concentration Camp and of the crematorium. I dreamed that I was a tied-up corpse awaiting my turn to be thrown into the crematorium. Human skeletons, for they were nothing else, were being dragged to the oven by iron pincers. The flames mounted gleefully. The bones were dry and brittle. A peppery fume filled my nose and throat. The "feeder's" skin peeled off with the hot breath of the furnace which scorched his sunken eyeballs. He would have liked to catch himself around the neck with the iron pincers and fling himself into the oven. Tall, healthy S.S. men stood around with whips and clapped their hands. They gave orders, laughed, and talked together. Now they brought along more "Muzlmanner" for the ovens. Suddenly, one of them stood up. He was deathly pale and had a deep wound on his forehead. I knew him. I also recognized his military shirt and medals. He snatched the pincers from the "heater" and wielded them right and left. He seized the SS men by the throat and flung them into the oven. They shrieked and fired at him. He cut through the cords that bound me, and he liberated all the women and children who were to be cremated.

"You are free. You are free!"

"Get up!"

My dream was abruptly interrupted by the Captain shouting, "Get up! Get up! Awaken! Make haste!"

They had brought in some badly wounded men. The Corporal and his men had come back with two dead and three dangerously hurt. The Corporal was one of the wounded, but it was a great victory — eleven prisoners and about four killed — Germans and "Wlasovtzes." The Corporal was wounded soon after the beginning of the fray. He said nothing about it to his men, carried on with superhuman strength, gave the orders, and not until it was all over did he collapse.

I rushed to his pallet-bed and washed the clotted blood off his face. It had soaked through the first-aid bandage and his shirt was stiff from it. My hands and fingers shook and my teeth chattered. I could not get out a single word. The Captain saw my distress and wanted to put me aside, but the wounded man made a gesture with his hand and said in simple Yiddish, "Let her be. Isn't she also a Jewish child?"

The Captain tried to question him, but he could not hear.

"Captain, I do not hear you. I seem to be deaf. I shall not be able to hear the joyful news of victory anymore, but I would like to live to see the last German soldier lying dead in the streets of Berlin. After that, I could die in peace, know that my mother. . . ." Here the Captain led me out of the room, for I had burst into weeping. Later I went in again with two sanitary assistants who put the Corporal on a stretcher and carried him into an improvised operating room. The Corporal asked, "Captain, am I then really so dangerously wounded?"

"Do not worry, all will be well. They will operate at once and more than one German will yet fall by your hand. "

"Yes, I have to live a little longer. We have not settled our account with them yet."

The Captain's reply had satisfied him.

An expected reinforcement, consisting of Russian soldiers, arrived. They encircled the district and cleared the woods of the enemy. The commanding officer, the Polkovnik (Colonel), a Russian in a leather jacket and a wadded cap, young, broad-shouldered, and good-tempered, listened to the men relate the story of the Corporal's attack on the armed bands. The sight of the four dead Germans filled him with enthusiasm.

"Eto-je, geroi! That's a hero!" he exclaimed. He then went into the operating room, greeted the Captain in comradely fashion, and inquired about the hero. The Captain pointed to the table on which the uncomplaining Corporal was lying. The Corporal's pulse quickened from one minute to the next, but his hands were as cold as ice. The Polkovnik asked the Captain's permission to note a few details. He turned to the Corporal and spoke, "Comrade, can you answer a few questions?"

"Yes," replied the Corporal, "only you must speak louder. I hear very faintly."

The Polkovnik asked questions in a firm even voice, and the Corporal answered.

"Your name?"

"Moses — in Yiddish — Moishe."

"Your father's name?"

"Abraham. "

"The family name?"

"Krause. "

"You were born?"

"On December 25, 1912, in Warsaw, in Zurawsky Street."

"Your nationality?"

"Jewish."

"Belonging to what Pary?"

"Jewish"

The Polkovnik explained that he would like to note if the Corporal had been a member of any Party.

The wounded man told him, "I am fully conscious of what I am saying, Comrade Polkovnik, so please put down; Party membership a Jew, a child of the Ghetto.

The Polkovnik was in a fit. The Captain glanced proudly at the Corporal.

"What relatives do you have?"

"I have a mother, Helena Krause, who is now living in Oktiubinsk."

"Should we let her know that you have been wounded?"

"No. It would be best, if it is possible, to tell my relatives in Palestine, in Eretz Israel, Rehovoth, Gluskin Street, Mr. Dov Krause."

"How long have you served with the Polish forces?"

"From May 15, 1943, from the first day of the formation of the Kosciusko Division.

"Were you wounded before?"

"Yes, near Lenino and Warsaw."

The Polkovnik wished to ask another question but the Captain signaled to him to be silent. Krause was gradually losing consciousness. The Captain accompanied the Polkovnik to the door. I stood glued to the table on which Krause was lying, and I heard him murmur, "Mame (mother) forgive me — please write to Eretz Israel, Rehovoth, Gluskin Street, Dov Krause — forgive me Mame."

Then, so I thought, he fell asleep.

The Captain came back. He collected Krause's medals, decorations, and military booklet, and placed them in an envelope. He wrote a note and handed Krause's things to me, saying sadly, "Take this to the office and tell them to send it to the Staff Office at once."

I took the note and the envelope to the Staff.

The Staff was located in the village of Hohenstein which was a half kilometer from the domain of Georgestal. On the way over, I made a mental note of the Palestinian address to which the notice of the Corporal's condition would be sent.

As I read, a dizziness came over me. My knees gave way, and I became covered with a cold sweat. I held onto the fence in order to keep from falling. I read the diagnosis and the Captain's addition to the military booklet,

"Shot through both lungs, died through loss of blood today, the. . . ."

So today, today, he fell asleep forever. Then why did they lie to him on the operating table? — simply to deceive him, to cheer him up? Of whom was his last thought? Why were they not supposed to let his mother know? Was it because he wanted Helena Krause in Oktiubinsk, his mother, to go on believing that he still lives? Maybe he really hoped to go on living, so why distress her needlessly? I remember what he said when they carried him to the operating table.

"Yes, Captain, we have not settled our account with them yet."

I returned from my errand to the Staff and I felt down and out. The Captain tried to cheer me, "We should have had more like those two, the one from Lodz and the one from

141

Warsaw! There would have been fewer for the Majdaneks and Auschwitzes."

I remembered my mother and little sister as well as the thousands I had seen taken to the gas-chamber. My dreams of the night before came back to me, and I felt, "Yes" as he said to us — "the four they killed in the woods would spill no more Jewish blood."

Three new graves were made near the one of Jacob Mandelbaum, the boy from Lodz. The soldiers transported the three dead men from the village to the woods. At the edge of the woods the truck stopped. The Captain and the Porutshnik (Lieutenant) of the battalion in which Krause had served, very quietly, without a word, lowered the young bodies into their graves. I looked at Moishe Krause's coffin — a simple wooden box, and could not restrain my tears. They led me aside. I did not hear the farewell words of the commanding officer and the others. And what, after all, are words?

The guard of honor sent a few salvo-shots into the air. The Officer read aloud the decision of the Staff to decorate the fallen. It all sounded silly to me. What could Moishe Krause want with medals now? Where is the medal equivalent to his lost life? Two crosses were laid on the graves of the fallen Christians. The Christian soldiers knelt beside them, and said a prayer for their fellow soldiers. On Krause's grave was laid a plain board with the inscription:

> CORPORAL OF THE POLISH ARMY
> MICHAEL KRAUSE
> SON OF ABRAHAM
> BORN 1912 IN WARSAW
> FALLEN ON MARCH 22, 1945
> HONOR HIS MEMORY.

His comrades had brought a few wreaths of wild greenery and laid them on the grave. Then came an order, "Take your places and march!"

Lonely and deserted, Krause and Mandelbaum were left lying in a dark woods on the detested German soil. No one said Kaddish for them, no one here will know anything about them.

❖ ❖ ❖

The time must be the last day of Passover.

A soft spring wind was blowing. The roads were crowded with armored cars, tanks, and troops which were moving on Berlin. Victory was in the air. The steel ring was closing in on Germany, the grip was being tightened, and the fighting became ever more desperate and cruel. Germany was defending herself with her last remaining strength like a wounded beast. Every day there were additional dead and injured. Our hands were full. I accompanied some wounded from Neugard and Platte to Schneidermuhl, the district where I had been a short time ago. I asked the chauffeur to drive through the village of Hohenstein. I wanted to have a last look at the graves of Krause and Mandelbaum. I picked some fresh wild flowers and made two little bunches to put on the graves, but the graves were no longer to be seen. The little stone heaps, having been trampled by horses and the wheels of gun-carriages were now level with the ground. Lying by the road side, I found the piece of board with the name of Corporal Michael Krause. I looked in vain for Mandelbaum's board. I took up Krause's board and I saw that the rain and passage of time had almost obliterated the dates and the names.

Melancholy overtook me. Will all remembrance of us also

be obliterated and disappear? But there was no time to stand and wonder, for the chauffeur signaled, and I had to drive on, away from them.

In my heart, I took a vow upon myself. If God will help me, and if I survive the war as I survived the concentration camp in Stutthof, I shall not forget them. I shall remember those two fallen Jewish soldiers, two out of thousands of heroic Jewish fighters who lie beside the roads of Europe, Africa, and Asia, and in mass-graves in countless places. They fought conscientiously to their last breath, defending the honor of our people.

Two of them, a son of Lodz and a son of Warsaw — we shall remember them for their sacrifice for their country, for their love for the Jewish people, for their hatred of our enemies, and for their courage.

Interviewed by Herman Taube
Translated by Helena Frank

MAJDANEK

O n a cold January morning, Volodia arrived in Lub-
lin, Poland. He walked down the train steps onto
the platform bedecked with Polish and red flags. The loud-
speakers announced that units of Marshall Ivan Koneff had
crossed the Narew River and punched out a salient between
Chechanow and Pomiechowek. "The conquest of Germany is
near."

It was snowing. Volodia loved the snowflakes under his
feet. More news came from the loudspeakers: "Armored N.
Divisions from Marshall Ivan Konev's Army overran Silesia.
General Eisenhower's Armies on the Duesseldorfer front
reached the Rhine River and are attacking from the Moselle
River to the north."

Volodia looked around the railroad. The platform was full
of Russian and Polish soldiers. There were German war pris-
oners in their green and light brown army coats. They looked
starved, holes in their cheeks, sunken eyes, rags bound on
their feet. He turned up his coat collar to protect himself from
the cold wind and together with two more passengers, stepped
onto a "Droshka" (A horse-drawn carriage) to Lublin.

The city of Lublin, the streets and old buildings were all
intact. The streets were full of people, women, children, sol-
diers arguing with the street vendors, older black-shawled
babushkas. Young girls leaning on soldiers' arms were strolling

in the snow, smiling. Volodia wondered at the difference in view from one of the devastated cities in Russia. The smell of hot cabbage and kelbasa hit his nostrils. He stepped into a small restaurant and sat at the far corner near the back door. A waitress came and took his order: a glass of warm milk and a piece of honey cake. He looked around the tables. People were drinking beer, lemonade, eating omelets, knockwursts, kelbasa, and were speaking in loud voices. Volodia looked for a familiar face, familiar eyes. There were none. He felt like a stranger here, an alien in his own country. He was glad to hear the Polish language, to walk on the snow on this soil, but the faces, the loud laughter of this throng of people, the old familiar curse words did not bring him any closer to the people here.

"Will I ever be able to break this distance and be one of them in the new Poland?"

Volodia paid and left the restaurant. He walked along the street in the snow still searching, looking for a face he would recognize as Jewish. A young, tall woman with laughing blue eyes walked by his side: "Would like to love me, Kochany?"

"No, dearie, I have to go to Majdanek."

"Jesus Maria! Why do you want to go there?"

She shrugged her shoulders and walked away in the snow.

Volodia hired a droshka and asked the driver to take him to Majdanek.

Volodia did not know what Majdanek was. All he was told was that he should go to an Army unit stationed near Lublin by that name. When his Evako-hospital advanced in the spring of 1944 into Ukraine and Belorussia, he heard of atrocities and mass murders committed by the Germans. He saw the mass graves and heard of deportations of whole communities to concentration and forced labor camps. However, he never heard of this murder factory six miles outside Lublin. He saw villages burned down, inhabitants murdered, hanged. He heard about Babi Yar, about terror and humiliation, of whole towns starved to death. Mass graves of women and children, the smell of decaying corpses followed him until the day he was wounded. When Majdanek was captured by the Red Army in July 1944, Volodia was in a Vitebsk Hospital half dead. Now, the shock was too much for him to bear. The gates looked like all army bases, fenced with barbed wire. A long line of civilians with travel bags on their backs were standing there waiting for the sentry to let them in. There were many Russian, American and French soldiers walking in and out of the gates. Volodia noticed some Jewish eyes among the crowd and he asked: "Amcho?"

"Yo!" they answered in Yiddish, "we just returned from Russia."

Volodia looked at their faces. They looked worse to him than the war prisoners he had seen in Lublin. Faces yellow and gray from tuberculosis, starvation, frostbit, wounds that had left holes in their skin, toothless jaws. However, their eyes had a gleam of hope. Volodia must have looked very ill to them. One man grabbed his arm: "Hey brother, you look terrible. You're bleeding from your mouth."

"It's nothing."

Volodia looked at the man. He was young, early twenties, gray haired, yellow skinned, a black-bluish frame around his eyes.

Volodia presented his documents to the officer at the inner gate. With his papers in his hand, he was sent to the Ambulatorium — the medical complex, a block of green barracks. He joined a group of newly arrived recruits and was marched to a barrack named "Bad und Disinfection" for a shower.

"In this concrete barrack," explained the accompanying sergeant, "the Germans gassed daily thousands of Jews with Zyklon gas. From there Zydys (Jews) were shipped by lorries to the crematoriums and mass graves."

So here he was, Volodia — Wolf Ben-Aharon Tarko, ready to take a shower and cleanse his body for service to the new Democratic Republic of Poland in a windowless barrack, where his people had died. And here were his fellow soldiers around him joking, making wisecracks. Their laughing made him tremble in convulsion.

Volodia picked up his new uniform with a Red Cross first aid kit of his own. He got a bed with a blanket and small pillow in a clean barrack near the Ambulatorium Building. He then went to the Mess Hall. It was crowded, thick with the warm steam and smell of cigarettes, smoked meats and sauerkraut. He walked into the Ambulatorium and asked the nurse for a glass of cold milk. Volodia pointed to his throat: "I have difficulties swallowing." The nurse came back with a deep dish of oatmeal and milk. Volodia was grateful.

"Thank you sister. I'm Vladislaw Tarko. I'm assigned to work with Major Gurewski in this ward."

"Oh good. We are short of help here. A lot of emergencies and we're short of everything, even bedpans. Some of the patients are so weak, they can't walk to the toilets. Oh, forgive me. I'm Sister Helena Janicka from Czestochowa. My father was a professional soldier."

"How did you get here?"

"In 1939, I went to look for my father who was a war prisoner in Belorussia."

"Did you find him?

"No, but I was arrested and sent to Siberia. I returned with the Polish Army. I have to go now. It was nice meeting you Vladislaw Tarko."

"Thank you for the kasha and milk."

Volodia worked the midnight shift. A truckload of Polish repatriates was delivered in the greatest secrecy after midnight. The doctor, medics and nurses on duty were shocked by what they saw. Only a few of the patients were able to walk in by themselves. The rest had to be helped or carried on stretchers. The orderlies put them up temporarily on cots and served tea with crackers. Volodia organized an emergency bath in a nearby barrack where they kept the Ambulatorium laundry. He worked all night cleaning up, shaving and disinfecting the poor repatriates. He then moved them back into beds in his ward. Volodia was exhausted, his throat was twitching with a gnawing pain, but the faces of these wounded repatriates were so shocking to him, that whatever he had seen in his years as a medic looked insignificant by comparison. He tried to talk to them, but to no avail. It seemed that their long experience in Russia made them fearful to say anything to the strangers in white, even if they spoke to them in Polish.

After duty, Volodia went back to his room. As tired as he was, he slept only a few hours. He walked around the green barracks. Something in him was pulling him again to the "Bad und Disinfection" barrack, like coming to the grave of his parents. The display was blood chilling. Volodia had to hold himself. He drew back in horror, walked around the barracks and returned in a few minutes following a crowd of people and listening to a guide describing Majdanek.

"The concrete barracks were served by 'polite' civilians. When the transports arrived, they invited the people to sit on benches to rest and leave their belongings. They undressed

149

here and were politely asked to step into the windowless bath-
house; first the men, then women and children. The dark
concrete boxes were locked and the gassing took place. First
some hot air was pumped in, then the Zyklon gas was show-
ered down on them. It took only a few minutes and two
hundred people were killed. One and a half million Jews died
here.

"Six gas chambers worked here constantly. From here, the
corpses were carried to the crematorium. The victims' belong-
ings were sorted here and shipped to Germany."

Volodia was trembling from the cold. He was hungry, but
he did not feel like eating. He went back to his barrack, took
his shoes off and laid down on his bed. He closed his eyes, but
he was awakened by a call to a paramedics orientation meet-
ing. Captain Szymanski provided information on personal
needs for active duty in the new frontier areas. The briefing
was short, no discussion, no questions. On the way out of the
session, a priest offered his thin hand to him.

"Tarko?"

"Father Gursky! Oh thank God!" The two men embraced.

"Chwala Bogu! You're alive! What happened to you?"

"Our ambulance was blown up by a mine. I was wounded."

"Are you all right now?"

"Thank God, still weak, but, thank God."

They walked slowly to the barracks. Father Gursky ap-
peared very thin in an oversized army coat he wore.

"Father, why don't you run along. It is nasty and I have to
walk slowly."

"Tarko," he said softly, "I have plenty of time. I'd rather
walk with you. Do you mind?"

Volodia's hands trembled when he opened the door.

"Please, come in."

"After you," Father Gursky said smiling.

It was dark in the barrack, cold, the wind blew through the window frames. Volodia took off his coat and shoes and laid down on his bed. Father Gursky did not utter a word. He just sat there, murmuring quietly to himself, "Holy Mary, Mother of God."

Volodia must have fallen asleep. His thoughts and now his dreams were the gas chambers, the repatriates, Garden-of-Eden Boulevard, Kyzyl Kishlak jail, Kursk mass graves. Volodia opened his eyes. Father Gursky stood beside his bed staring sadly at him.

"Tarko, how do you feel now?"

"What did I do?"

"You kept pleading, 'God, where are you?' "

"Where is He, Father Gursky? Where was He when all this around here happened?"

"Tarko, He is here with us. He returned us from the most remote corners of the Soviet Union, a crowd of ragged and hungry, sick and humiliated people. We're joining together to rebuild our country, our army, our shattered beliefs. God is with us, Tarko. Our country will rise again. We must hope. We're going to be free again."

Father Gursky sat on his bed, tired and said. "Talk to me."

Volodia could not find a word to say. His soul, his heart was empty. He had no energy to get up when he was called to duty.

Volodia worked all night in the Ambulatorium — a hospital in miniature. Orderlies and nurses rolled stretchers in and out. Doctors were working around a metal operating table. The corridor was full of waiting wounded soldiers.

Volodia fed the patients who were unable to move their

hands and helped them to the lavatories. He felt in a daze and moved as if asleep, dreaming. Soon things fell out of his hands. His white coat was red with blood. He did not remember eating anything that day. His legs hurt, but he managed to work through the night. He went back to his barrack. Soldiers, officers greeted him, but Volodia felt isolated, withdrawn. The only thing he felt he had in common here was the "Bad und Disinfektion" chamber.

After a week of briefings and lectures about the Kosciuszko Division, after parades and sermons. Volodia got an assignment to the Polish Army hospital in Neugard, a small town on the frontier near Stettin. He was also given thirty days leave to go anywhere he wished. He questioned going back to Lodz. Father Gursky had told him that all the Jews of Lodz had died in Chelmno, Auschwitz, Ravensbrook, and Sackshausen. The last Jews of Lodz Ghetto were murdered and buried in mass graves on January 17, two days before the Russian Armies entered the city.

"Maybe there were some Jews left, hidden somewhere."

"I walked in the ghetto streets . . . nothing except rats, flies, and corpses." Father Gursky was depressed. "All my family killed, deported to Germany. They robbed our hospital clean."

"I still would like to go. I must."

"God be with you, Tarko."

Before leaving, Volodia went to the "museum" again. He had to go, as much as it grieved him. Again he followed a group of Russian officers and listened to a guide, a middle-aged civilian, gray-haired and gray-faced, explaining the system of the death factory. "Only a few minutes and they were gone."

They! They! They! Volodia's imagination saw his family, his grandparents, uncles, aunts, neighbors, his girlfriend and her parents. They all were "they" and they had perished here, or in Chelmno, Auschwitz. What other camps had Father Gursky mentioned? Volodia still suffered from a loss of hearing and temporary blackouts. Nevertheless, he followed the Russians and the guide to the end. They all walked on a field where white ashes had melted the snow. They stepped on bits of bones, skulls. The guide expertly explained, "A layer of manure and then the cabbage seeds — good *capusta*. It is used to feed our soldiers now."

Volodia felt as if someone were strangling him. "For a week now you've eaten borscht and cabbage soup fertilized by the ashes of your own people," he cried to himself.

He followed the group to the crematorium and the furnaces. The smell of carbol and the odor of decomposed human bodies was still there.

"Normally," the guide explained, "two thousand bodies were burned here daily, but the Germans were not satisfied. They were eager to kill more, so they shot and burned whole transports of men, women, and children outside in the woods. They sprinkled gasoline over them and set them afire while many of them were still alive."

A Russian officer walked away bewildered and started shouting, "Filthy Fascist murderers! I will kill! I will kill the sons-of-bitches! *Yey Bogu* — By God!"

"I knew I would find you here. Come on, I'll take you back to your barracks." Father Gursky took his arm and led him away.

"Tarko, are you awake?"

"Yes, Father."

"Why are you sitting in the dark?"

"My eyes hurt."

"We've had enough darkness in our lives, haven't we?"

"We still have."

"With the Lord's help, we will see the light soon."

"Where is the Lord? In *Disinfektion Kammer II?*"

"He is in you."

"I am death and so is He."

"So why did you come here?"

"I hoped God was still alive."

"He is Tarko, He is."

"Where? In the barrels of human fat? In the mountains of children's shoes, in the mountain of ashes? Perhaps in Chopin Warehouse among the balls of human hair?"

"Tarko, I understand. You're tired and sick, but this is not the way to think and feel. You're a Jew, the eternal Jew who survived the Romans, the crusades, the Russian Czars, the Bolsheviks, and now the Nazis. I heard in Lodz that your people fought back in Warsaw, Vilna, Bialystok. They had nothing to fight with and fight for, but they did fight back. Now, on the threshold of a new beginning, you don't want to live? Tarko, what's happened to your spirit? We are winning this war, victory is near. I remember you used to quote from the Sayings of the Sages, 'By force you must live.'"

"I cheated and fooled my patients, my wounded soldiers. I don't believe in it."

"It helped your patients, it helped me. Many times I was thinking of you."

"One and a half million people died here. Why? Why?"

"I don't know the answer. Ten thousand Polish officers died in Katyn. Hundreds of thousands died in Warsaw, in Siberia, in German Labor camps. Why?"

"Why do people kill each other?"

"They are blind with hatred. God forgive them."

"God needs forgiveness himself. Where was He when all this happened?"

"Tarko, can I turn on the lights?"

"I don't care."

Father Gursky switched on the light bulb.

"Jesus Maria! Look at yourself!"

The pillow was soaked with the blood coming out of Volodia's mouth.

"What did you do?"

"Nothing. My wound is bleeding."

"Why did you come here? Why didn't you stay in the hospital?"

"I wanted to go the front . . . to kill Nazis."

"You never killed before, did you?"

"I will now, until I die."

"Stop talking. Don't move."

Father Gursky ran out of the barrack and returned with Sister Helena Janicka. "Please, come with us."

Sister Helena and Father Gursky helped him get up and walked him to the ambulatorium. Major Gurewski, a stocky man, gray-haired and pale, chatted with Father Gursky, "This exhibit of Nazi bestiality should not be shown to wounded soldiers. I am here two months and still can't look at that inferno." Dr. Gurewski gave Volodia an injection to stop the bleeding. Sister Helena came back with a clean khaki shirt.

"Did you eat anything today?" Dr. Gurewski asked in a friendly voice.

"No, Major Gurewski. I don't feel hungry today. I saw the Jew-cabbage fields."

Dr. Gurewski swallowed hard.

"What do you feel like?"

"Drowsy. "

Father Gursky helped him back to his barrack. The injection started working and in minutes Volodia was asleep.

When Volodia woke up, Father Gursky was at his bedside.

"Feel better, Tarko?"

"Yes."

"Here is some cold tea."

"Is that all a base chaplain has to do? Watch over me?"

"I'm partly responsible for making a medic out of you, remember?"

"Oh yes. I remember and I'm thankful"

"I spoke to Major Gurewski and he said the sooner you leave this place, the better off you'll be."

"When can I leave?"

"As soon as you feel a little stronger."

"If I survived *Disinfektion Kammer II,* I'm the strongest man on this planet."

"Stop talking about it. Look to tomorrow. Forget the horror."

"Never! I will live with it forever."

"I'm sorry for them. How dare we forget?"

"You must if you want to live."

"Who said this world is worth living in?"

"You must live. There are so many wounded. They need you."

"Forgive me for being so bitter. I was so glad you were here when I woke up."

Father Gursky had a smile on his face. "Are you going directly to Pomerania?"

"No. I have four weeks leave. I'm planning to visit some friends."

Father Gursky whispered, "Holy Mary. I hope you find them, someone."

"I hope so too.

"I hope we meet someday, Tarko, in a better world."

"God willing, Father Gursky. You gave me courage."

"You gave me my confidence back as a servant of my faith."

"You know that I am of another faith."

"No, you're wrong. We are all of one creed, one belief. We are all children of one Heavenly Father."

Volodia stretched out his hands. "Please help me get up."

This excerpt from Herman's Taube's novel Red Village *centers on a Polish Jew serving in the Polish army, first in a hospital in Soviet Asia and later in Europe. In this episode, the protagonist returns to Poland for assignment to a Polish army unit of the Majdanek death camp, recently taken from the Nazis. He arrives in January, 1945, unaware of the enormity of the Nazi slaughter of the Jews.*

Poems

❖ ❖ ❖

Berlin, Savoy Hotel

The bathroom at the Savoy Hotel
is immaculately brushed, spotless.
The toilet seats are furnished with
a rotary motor that cover the seats
with fresh towels after every flush.

Mr. Gantz, a native Berliner, who
lives in Haifa, Israel, came back to
his place of birth, after an absence of
49 years, invited by Berlin's City Senate,
is hesitant to sit down and use the toilet.

As we leave the lavatory, he shares
with me some thoughts and memories:
"On Kristallnacht, November 9,1938
I was arrested and taken to Buchenwald
with my father and my younger brother.

"The latrine barrack was awash with feces,
we stood in line deep in human excrement,
my brother, weakened by dysentery, fell off
the plank into the deep ditch. I tried to
help him. The guard hit me with his whip.

"I returned to my barrack soaked with blood,
my father washed my face and kept asking:
'Where is my son?' I lied: 'They took him away.'
My father died crawling on his hands and knees
in the torture chambers of Buchenwald."

"Mr. Gantz," I asked, "why did you come to Berlin?"
"My spouse insisted we visit the cemetery here,
my mother is also buried here. Fortunately, she
died before Kristallnacht. Doesn't it sound silly?
I can't use the hotel toilet. Too deep the scars."

Berlin 1987

Stadtfest Berlin

She insisted that they will visit
the Historical Yearmarket Fest,
listen to a musical presentation
of the Grafenauer Spitzbuben from
her grandfather's family village
she visited so often as a child.

The biergarden was full of people,
young and old, tourists and natives.
She sat there enjoying the crowd,
when suddenly her face turned pale.
She recognized someone she knew,
she remembered his Nazi uniform.

He sat there with grandchildren,
his daughter-in-law and his son,
an exact image of the old man, how
he looked 50 years ago. He was
the hunter and she was the hunted.
Now the perpetrator and victim met.

Please, let us leave, I'm suffocating.
The music was playing "Unser Heimat,"
the crowds leisurely strolled around
the exhibit booths, eating ice cream,
drinking beer. Only she was running,
mumbling: "What am I doing here?"

Berlin 1987

Lodz

Lodz. I was lonely,
cold, hungry, unhappy.
Why do I remember you
so affectionately?

Lodz. My girlfriend
is not there anymore.
Why do I long for the
home where I grew up?

On my street of cobble
stones there were no
trees on the sidewalks.
Why do I dream of flowers?

I grew up with no friends,
no toys, no place to play.
The only game I knew was
gazing at the stars, the moon.

After school I studied
with my grandfather, he
was killed during the war.
In my dreams he's still here.

In my dreams my city Lodz,
my girlfriend, my grandfather
they are all alive and well.
Only I alone am dead. . . .

June 1987

The Sound of the Trumpeter

On the last day of October
the heaven over Krakow looks
a morbid gray, almost depressing.
The cloudiness casts a shadow on
the medieval castle on Wawel Hill.

A group of Russian officers
at a nearby table drink vodka,
their loud voices drowning out
the sound of church bells that
makes the Poles feel insecure.

The Poles grumble and worry
about their future: "You tourists
from America think we are free.
Three decades after victory,
the Russians are still here."

The sound of a trumpeter comes
from the Church of St. Mary.
We can see the golden cross
from the restaurant window
despite the heavy overcast.

The sound of the trumpeter's
hejnal breaks abruptly, is
stilled and then continued.
We wondered loudly why Poland
can't choose a better player.

Our Polish guide, a teacher,
explained to us the reason
why the sound of the trumpeter
breaks abruptly and continues
after a moment of silence:

In the Thirteenth Century,
Poland was threatened with
disaster from Genghis Khan,
The mongol hordes under Ogadai
swept Europe and reached Krakow.

The armies of the Khan came
to the Vistula River and moved
toward Krakow after burning
and ruining cities and villages,
killing everyone on their path.

One day, when the trumpeter climbed
to his post on the church tower,
he saw the dust of the approaching
Khan horsemen attacking the gates.
He sounded an alarm on the trumpet.

A Mongol warrior drew his bow
and the arrow swiftly hit the heart
of the trumpeter. He wavered,
tried to continue playing but
the sound was stilled forever.

For many generations after, the
trumpeters of Krakow have kept

this tradition. Not the Nazis,
not the Russians ever succeeded
in stilling the broken notes.

This moment of silence is a sign
of Poland's spirit and hope for freedom.
Someday, when Poland will really be free,
the trumpeter will sound the hejnal
song unbroken, clear, straight, free. . . ."

Krakow, October 1975

The Girls of the Warsaw Ghetto

A written order was delivered to the Judenrat:
"One hundred young girls, pretty and healthy,
must surrender by midnight to the Gestapo."
The Militia, the guards and Military Police
hastened to the Bais Yaakov Schol, grabbing
young girls. Without saying farewell to their
parents or teachers, they were loaded on army trucks
and taken to a hostelry at the military barracks.

A blitz-woman of the SS addressed the girls:
Don't cry lucky frauleins, you were chosen to
entertain handsome men of a superior race.
You will be dressed and fed, and sleep on soft beds
with clean sheets, bedcovers of satin, silk pillows,
you will drink sweet wine, dance to Wagnerian music.
Our soldiers will treat you gently, you just behave.
After showers you will receive new, elegant attire.

The girls undressed and went to the showers.
They turned on the faucets and let the water run.
All of them took a poison they carried.
While dying they hugged and said their prayers. . . .
They left a note, "We died clean. Pray for our souls".
Here ends the ballad of ninety-two Jewish students,
mourned by their families, remembered for eternity:
Ninety-two Jewish girls "who died clean."

A Letter to a Friend

To Isaac Bashevis Singer

For four decades now I have read your books,
your language is subtle, rich, clear, beautiful —
a juicy pomegranate. Your Yiddish vocabulary is
full of real pearls, priceless word jewels.
Even your nymphs, naiads, ghosts, dybbuks
are a great delight to read and remember.
You created powerful characters, renegades
and pious, ordinary and supernatural.
Your tales have their roots in the past:
Believers who live like savages,
strangers who are kindhearted and tolerant.
Most of your stories close in sadness,
wicked or holy end up disillusioned,
overpowered by pain, grief and wiped out.
You knock down old walls of ghetto slums,
facing your readers with the primitive life,
the superstitious customs of the past.
You convinced us to burn down old walls
but you failed to show us a new road,
useful values, new ground we can build on.
The post-Holocaust era has nothing to offer,
the modern world is wild, worthless, vanity,
their new culture — a heap of rubbish,
not worth reading, not worth listening to.
What are we to do — descendants of the shtetls?
We are left in a desert of thin sand.

Vermin

I heard it almost every day:
You Jews are all vermin, shit.
Rage ran through my veins,
I became a ravening animal.

First we'll kill the Germans,
then we'll dispose of the shit:
all that is left of the Zydys.
Poland must be free of this scum.

The only good Zydys are dead ones.
We are called murderers, hooligans,
so be it. We'll use their ashes
to fertilize our fields, our crops.

I carried no gun, only a medic's bag,
a big red cross on my arm and cap,
my army uniform smeared with blood,
mud, like my unshaven, fatigued face.

I wondered daily if they would kill me,
I said nothing when I heard them talk.
I did my work, giving first aid, helped
the same soldiers that called me shit.

I knew then, if I would survive this war,
I'll never be able to live in Poland.
In the war I was fighting for my people,
now, let the Poles live with their own shit.

In Retirement

Silent phone:
Preposterous
muteness, quiet
as in a tomb.

I sit and wait
at my desk for
someone to call,
to hear a sound.

A familiar voice,
a laugh to rejoice,
a cry for sad news,
some sort of flirt.

A dirty, sordid joke?
A salesman's pitch?
A recorded prayer?
Sorry. Wrong number?

A donation request?
An obscene call?
My phone is silent:
A monk in seclusion.

December 5, 1989

A Letter

To Merrill Leffler

Look between the lines of my "poetic notes" —
a vocabulary of distorted, undisciplined verse.
You will find them all lacking skill, uncanny,
flavorless like a bowl of Chinese noodles.

Yet beyond the inadequate words you will see
an exposed soul in constant grapple to rid myself
from the terror of dreadful memories, nightmares,
always in struggle to control my equilibrium.

I feel like a caged animal trying to get away
from daily flashbacks that fluctuate in my mind,
from panic to anger, fighting to overcome anxiety
and free myself from the tremors of fright.

I am a stranger in my own home, the bright rooms
look dark like storage space in our building,
a vague fear makes me feel insecure, thinking:
the Holocaust is hiding in every closet.

When I see flashing lights, hear whistles, alarms,
or unexpected knocks on my door, I get suspicious,
my heart is sinking, thinking the Nazis are
coming again. Will I resist? Will I oblige?

It worries me to listen to the news. Will bombs
jostle the earth again, squashing humanity like
worms? I am burdened by sacrilegious thoughts:
Our Heavenly Father, will He once more be silent?

172

Look beyond my words, see the pain of my chained soul.
I carry the load of my lost people, my generation,
I am the voice and the shadow of their memory.
Shadows cannot always portray clear, vivid pictures.

July, 1986

Autumnal Sunset

The last light vanishes on the horizon,
evening shadows come out from their hiding,
a cool, homeless wind looks for cover in the
branches outside my foggy windows.

Spiderweb and brown leaves glide in the air.
Carried by the wind, falling to the ground,
they surrender their beaut to the season,
fluttering down to the wet, rotten grass.

I join the swaying trees in evening prayer.
It's getting cold now as the traffic slows,
it rains. A crow on a naked branch cries
of the loss of summer. So do I, so do I.

Poem

"All those that are born, with great horror behold."
Zalman Shneiur

My daughters, Miriam, Judy, and Adele,
when we get together, we haven't done
more than say hello to each other.
My aging process developed in a gap
that I find very frightening and saddening.

Sometimes my chest pains cause a
panic situation, it affects my self
confidence. I feel old age catching up.
I feel like calling you, speaking to you,
but, difficult to explain, I run from it.

I try to analyze my feelings, my behavior,
maybe this has something to do with love
for you all, not to say anything sad.
For the same reason I don't complain to
your mother. I am going around in circles.

Now, the older I get, the more I need you,
I need the presence of my grandchildren.
I know, I sinned: I devoted too much of my
life to society work, to culture and writing,
this is not something I regret doing.

Now, getting older, I look around and see
that what really counts is not just music,
arts, social standing, and my writings.
I need the closeness of you.
It is getting colder as I get older. . . .

Cholesterol

For seventy years I lived dangerously:
hunger, war, strenuous work, overweight,
open-heart surgery, too-low blood pressure.
Happily I reached retirement, rest arrived,
time to go out to a good restaurant,
to attend charitable and social functions.
Caution. A crisis has arisen: Cholesterol.

I must go on a diet, no red meat, no cheese,
no full milk, no white challa, no chocolate,
no cake, no sodas, no alcoholic beverages, no
pretzels, maximum daily calories: 1,800.
Now I live on cereal, yogurt and one coffee.
Every time I desire a cookie, ice-cream, an egg,
I think of Cholesterol. I grumble: What a life.

I have become an expert on diastolic hypertension,
elevated blood Cholesterol and the risk factor.
The adverse effect of obesity on the elderly,
and the required therapy: limit the intake of
food, alcohol, stop smoking, omit depression.
Failure to obey the rules can cost you your life.
I'm in distress just thinking of Cholesterol.

Tales and Fables

Some poets are grandfathers
with the souls of children,
they believe that Solomon was
the wisest king on earth,
they are convinced that the
Messiah will come in our days,
on a Friday afternoon to Safad,
a town in the hills of Galilee.
He will descend from Mount Meron
on his way to Jerusalem.
They dream of discovering
one of the thirty-six righteous
people — on whose good deeds
the survival of our world depends.
They live on tales and fables about
Asmodeus and four-eyed monsters
and honestly believe in the legend
that Adam sacrificed a unicorn
on an altar that is now Jerusalem.
They dream of monsters having heads
of a calf, one eye in their hearts
and a horn on their foreheads.

I myself think often about Cain:
that originally our Mother Earth
was flat, unwrinkled. Only after the
Earth received the blood of Abel,
it became mountainous, full of quakes.
Having seen so many Cains murder

millions of Abels in my generation,
hearing in my dreams the Abels weeping,
I started to believe that all misfortunes,
epidemics, diseases, are the result of
the wicked Cains living among us.
I know it is naive to think this way.
I can't help it. I am one of the poets
with this primitive mind, who believes
he has actually seen these Cains and Abels.

August 8, 1987

Autumn Love

Traffic lights outside my window
reflect in the ceiling of our bedroom.
Like huge flashlights they fall
on my pillow, startling and
awakening me like an alarm clock.

This morning I found your head
resting on my arm.
You were still deep asleep
breathing heavily, making a sound
like groaning, but you were smiling.

Quietly I touched your hair,
I listened to your silent lament.
Outside our windows a new day
came gliding in our bedroom
with a sound of a crouching wind.

Your sighing stopped and you awoke:
What will the weather be today?
They predict the first snowfall
of the season, but who cares?

Outside the heaven is full of clouds
but inside the house is warm,
I feel like spring, all because
this morning I found your head
resting in my arms.

December 5, 1985

A Prayer of Zalman Wassertzug

"I called on the Lord in my distress,
the Lord answered me."
                    Psalm 118

I have been afraid of death and oblivion,
I was frightened by my fragility and aloneness,
until I realized that this is the nature of life,
that all of us are destined to become fragile
when we reach a certain age.

I thank You Lord for the blessing You have given
me to build a decent life here on this earth.
All I ask You now is to give me enough energy
to live my remaining days in peace, to be able
to understand, to hear, to breathe, to recognize
the people who are dear to me, care about me.

I know that there are hardships I must endure.
I cannot brush away the nightmares and memories
of the dear ones I lost. But I realize that lapse
of memory, decline in health is part of getting old.

Sometime I doze off and dream about my past,
my childhood, my family, I recognize faces, but
don't remember their names. This makes me sad.
I pray inwardly that you will give me strength
to accept myself with all my limitations.

That the people around me will not judge
me harshly when I am experiencing anger, rage.

Finally, I pray, when the time will come to die,
You will let me leave this world with dignity.

As for now I pray that You let me spend my days
without grief and pain, without anxiety and fear.
Lord. All I ask of You is to give me inner peace.

Hebrew Home, Rockville, Maryland

Confessions of One More Sin

After Mariv and Havdalah,
unburdened of sin, mind at peace,
we gather outside our synagogue
for Kiddush-Levana, facing the moon.

To the music of David Shneyer's guitar,
hand in hand we dance and sing, sway
with a spirit encompassing body and soul.
The radiance of faces expresses harmony.

On my way home I hum a melody,
thinking of the tradition, the custom
to build a Sukkah after the fast-break.
I realized my wish is futility.

I feel strangely lonely, a let-down —
who will sit in the Sukkah with me?
Our children grown, gone away from it,
completely out of my religious heritage.

In the chanting of the *Al Chets*
when repeating committed transgressions
I failed to add once more, I'm guilty
for my children's estrangement.

October 7, 1984

Lazar Manes Complains

Subconsciously I bow down at *Borchu*,
just as I bow down at *Anachnu Korim*.
But when it comes to say *Kaddish*
my mind and lips are sealed tightly,
like the Gates of Heaven were closed to
the cries of my two children I remember now.

My lips refuse to say "Yisgadal Ve'yiskadash."
When our enemies tormented my wife,
You were nowhere to be found — You,
who reigned supreme in my home.
We worshipped You, dedicated our souls
to the sanctification of Your name.

Why were we treated so ungratefully?
Why did You allow our children to be murdered?
Where was Your mercy, Your justice?
I hope that someday I will be able
to understand Your ways, Your absence
while millions needed You.

Until then, I'll continue to say my prayers
inwardly, with sealed lips, like
a son whose father turned away his face
from his child in a perilous time.
You are still my father because I love You,
need and adore You. Still it hurts so much.

Yom Hashoah, 1987

The Days of Awe

I need a day to repent my sins,
I need an hour to confess my faults,
I need a minute for reconciliation
with my God, and a lifetime to make up
with my relatives, neighbors, friends.

I need a day for solemn prayers,
I need an hour for remembrance,
I need a minute to hear the Shofar,
I need a lifetime for works of mercy.
All days of my life are days of Awe.

The Heavenly Gates are always open.
In communal charity work, in support
for the elderly, aid to the needy,
there is my salvation: helping my
people reconciles me with God.

Every day is a day of repentance,
every hour is a good time for prayer,
every night is a moment of judgment,
a self-examination of our conscience.
What good did I accomplish today?

I will not wait until Rosh Hoshanah
to seek forgiveness of someone I have
hurt, offended, did not respond to his
or her call for help. Today is the day.
There are no scapegoats to bear my sins.

There is no Temple, no Holy of Holies,
my heart is my altar where God rests,
my home is my sanctuary and the place
where I practice lovingkindness and
pray for God's forgiveness and blessing.

Pain and Fear

"Blest who can unconcern'dly find
Hours, days, and years slide soft away
In health of body, peace of mind,
Quiet by day. Sound sleep by night."
                              Alexander Pope

At the threshold of my "senior years"
I'm experiencing varying effects of pain.
I learned to disregard and dispel the
pangs that irritate my spine and neck.
I learned how to cope with discomfort
during World War II: they removed
bits of shrapnel from my body when I was
rescued from an ambulance that was hit
by a mine and exploded. My ulcerations
lasted nine months, the suffering continues.

When I read of people who die in their sleep,
I am jealous: I am not afraid that I will die,
I'm remarkably calm when thinking of death.
What scares me is a prolonged disease.
Will the nightmares of the war overwhelm
my mind, my thoughts? Will I be able to resist
the scenery of the Holocaust wracking my dreams?
They are more horrifying and painful than
the irritation and discomfort in my bones
when I try to coddle myself in my blanket.

I dream of dark pits and crawling out of them
becomes more difficult as I get older,

my resistance weakens when I creep upwards
and drop back down to the bottom of the crater.
I feel helpless, I stopped struggling, screaming,
no one on the top listens to my call anyhow.
I am scared of the deaf ears around me,
I fear the loneliness, resignation, helplessness,
that is still prevalent in my world today.
I am not afraid to die, what I fear is despair.

April, 1986

The Night after the Battle

A ghostly silence
hangs over the valley,
the cool night breeze
spreads a scent of
burning flesh.
The lament of animals
and humans died down,
all we can see in
the darkness is a
reflection of the moon
in a red stream of blood
that comes from the
valley, circles around
and around and flows
to nowhere, nowhere.
Our crew works in silence,
we carry the dead
stepping with our boots
deep into the red stream.
Only our head nurse
weeps quietly, inwardly:
she was born and raised
in this valley.
All night long we carried
the fallen, all night
our head nurse cried.
In the morning, weary,
our black-haired nurse

fell silent. His eyes
lost their glow,
her hair and eyebrows
turned gray.

Night Thrust

They moved fast and silently
like ghosts in the night,
across corn and thicket fields
toward the edge of the forest.
Suddenly they found themselves
facing an enemy vigilante patrol,
so close that they all almost
scraped against their three-wheeler
motorcycles and motor-sleds.
The smell of baked potatoes and
fried fish and the resting men
around an expiring bonfire
was both scaring and thrilling.
They opened fire and killed
the roaring mad, surprised patrol.
The partisans grabbed the carbines,
machine guns, leftover food,
bottled drinks and disappeared.
A roar of army trucks briskly
advanced toward the encampment.
The partisans retreated
into the forest. They faded away like
shades in the night, walking in
silence, reloading their carbines,
caressing their new machine guns
like men fondling the girlfriends
they were longing for for a long time.

December, 1944

Uzbekistan

My kibitka room was a two-by-two,
the walls and floor made of mud,
I slept on a rug infested by insects,
often awakened by scorpion stings.

Every morning, when the sun appeared
over the snow-bedecked mountains,
I was awakened by the melodious tune
coming from horns on top of a mosque.

I washed my face in an arik, a little
stream behind my kibitka, ate some yogurt,
dry fruits, urugs and drank hot tea.
In minutes I was at work in our clinic.

The days were long, the work exhausting,
but not the heat that wore us out;
the lack of medical supplies, food and
field beds was upsetting and depressing.

Yet we worked with vigor and devotion,
we knew a war was going on in Europe
against a mutual enemy and the sick here
were the relatives of the fighting soldiers.

Every evening, on the way back home,
I listened to the radio loudspeaker
blaring the news from the front lines.
I was envious of the fighting men.

Until one day I was called to the Militia
and given papers to Saratow Polish Army.
I said Salaam to my kibitka and my friend
at the Malaria Clinic. They and I cried.

Partisan Guide Book

As a young boy he spoke Yiddish,
in school he learned Polish and Hebrew,
when he escaped to the Soviet Union
he intensely studied Russian.
When he joined the partisans and
was sent as a deviationist behind
enemy lines, he learned German.

From a pocket-size guide book he learned
phrases like Waffen hinlegen, Ergieb dich!
Halt! Bei Fluchtversuch wird geschossen!
The small book was a treasury of instructions
on how to use firearms, the best ways of wrecking
enemy trains, trucks, motorcycles and how
to survive on a diet of moss, bark, and snow.

In the forest at night they listened to the
news, sang songs and read the guide book.
The songs were about Zoya Kosmodemianskaya,
who was executed by the enemy in the village
of Petrishchevo, followed by a chapter
on how to attack the enemy lines from the rear,
how to destroy enemy garrisons at night.

One day the partisan guide book vanished.
Someone ran out of machorka paper and felt
that he knew already enough about sabotage.
Mischa, who knew the booklet by heart, became
the politruk of the partisan otriad-unit.

Every night, after returning from an attack
on enemy positions he was rereading from memory.

His fame reached Moscow and orders came that
he be transferred to other partisan regions
to teach them the art of blowing up railways,
bridges, trains. One night, when attacking a
caravan of German trucks carrying food supplies,
Mischa was wounded. His fellow partisans were sad,
but Mischa cheered them up. It was not in vain.

The next morning Mischa was taken to a village
and left there under the care of a "contact."
The comrade who carried him to the village
cried when he said goodbye to his politruk.
"Mischinka dorogoi, I make my confession now.
It was I who took our partisan guide
and used it for cigarette paper for the rest of us."

Platte (Ploty) Pomerania, May 1945

Brenda — the Partisan

For Brenda Senders

The cannonade continued all day,
several men were hit by flying shells,
a woman died from loss of blood.
They were besieged by an unseen enemy
wrestling with death in bitter cold.
They tried to get away from the forest
having no more food, little water, scarce arms.
Twice they sent scouts to find a way out,
they came back breathless, tired, shaking,
overcome by the bitter cold and constant
fire coming from all sides.

The commander of the partisan group
decided to find out who was doing the shooting.
Brenda, a girl of eighteen volunteered.
She armed herself with hand grenades,
scrambled out of the forest under night cover
and came to the close-by village.
She did not detect any military vehicles,
no German units, all chalupas were dark.
With one hand on her pistol, her fur hat
pulled down over her forehead, she pounded
on the first window at the edge of the village.

A sleepy figure of an old woman appeared
at the door looking bewildered like a child:
"What are you looking for in the wee hours?"
"I am looking for my muzhik. He went to

see the Germans and did not come back.
Can you tell me where the soldiers are?"
"There are no army units in our village."
"Who is assaulting the forest all day?"
"A bunch of Reds are hiding in the woods,
our men are trying to clear them out.
You'll find your man at the big house."

Brenda was astonished by her discovery.
She waited until daybreak in the yard
of the house at the edge of the village.
Men appeared, loading a horse-drawn wagon
with explosives, food, water, cartridge chains,
small machine guns and hand-grenades.
A German officer commanded the group
of the armed civilians who stepped in line.
Swiftly, Brenda pulled with her teeth
the pins of the hand grenades and tossed them
on the wagon and on the group.

The wagon exploded, hurling bodies in the air.
Screaming, blasts of broken glass, horse shrill
filled the air. Villagers came running.
Brenda heard the crowd lamenting: The Lord
punished us for killing innocent people.
Fire devoured the chalupa and near-by dwellings.
In the confusion Brenda left the village,
back to her partisan group in the forest.
That morning, after burying the woman,
the group left for another hiding place
on the outskirts of the Sarna woodlands.

To Anita

I will gather all the flowers
and braid a wreath for you to
take to Auschwitz — Birkenau.

I will conceal them in a large
vase overflowing with my tears,
waiting for decades to burst out.

You will leave the flowers at
the Jew-Block 27 in Auschwitz.
If the doors are locked, as usual,
take the vase to the Birkenau Camp.

Leave them in any one of the barracks,
all the prisoners there were my people.
Neither time nor distance will make us
forget or forgive their martyrdom.

November 13, 1987

Loneliness

Loneliness makes us sad
and sad people are lonely.
They hide behind four walls,
withdraw to nowhere.
The only voice they hear
is outside breathing;
inside is dullness, impotence.

A shadow hovers around them,
makes their minds freeze,
depresses their senses
to a slow, self-destruction;
they don't move, afraid to
disturb the ghost of desolation.

Aimlessly they sit like frozen
corpses, pretend to read, think.
But their minds are blank.
All they feel is unconscious
weakness, repudiation of will
to live, to love, to smile.

They have notions, illusions
that, perhaps, they will die,
their dreams are pure vanity.
They go on living in desolation
and make their friends sad.

On Memorial Day

I sat beneath an oak tree
in the rear of my house,
holding a blank sheet of paper
on my lap, waiting for the muses.
I was gazing at the moon
the night light of God's garden,
inhaling cool air, aroma of grass,
mingled with the odor of
fried fish coming from my
neighbor's yard. The muses weren't
coming . . . I shut my eyes.
I let the wind take me on
the wings of my dreams
to far away places, to the stars
where phones don't ring,
no clocks to watch,
no newspapers to read
about violence, politics.
Like a spider's silk, the stillness
built a net around me,
I hear the trees whisper prayers,
the faint cry of crickets.
The green lawn under my feet
turns into a carpet.
Like a lunatic I walk upwards
on this green carpet to the stars.
I was awakened by my wife
muttering from an upstairs window:
"Where are you? Are you asleep?

Come up and watch television."
I looked at the screen.
"Sheerest nonsense, I haven't missed
a great deal," I said.
"Certainly not," she answered,
"just that I want you in the house,
I want you to sit beside me."
My conscience felt guilty.
Here we are waiting for a day
of rest, to honor valor,
    to remember their spirit,
        the sacrifice for kin and country,
and here,
I am flying to the stars,
waiting to write poems
noticing the cry of crickets
and not seeing my lonely wife. . . .
We fell asleep holding hands.

The Grocer on Warner Street

The shrill of sirens pierces the air,
dogs bark, cats weep all night.
Outside the bar across the street
drunkards sing and curse loudly.
He crawls under the cover, tries to sleep,
his five-year old daughter pulls his arm
crying. She is afraid of the dark,
does not want to sleep in her bed,
she is seeing monsters outside the window.
While her mother goes downstairs for milk
and a cookie, he tries to calm her:
"There is nothing to be afraid of,
all the windows have iron bars."
He holds her in his arms and worries:
What takes her so long downstairs?
The minutes are like long hours,
he thinks of sharp pointed knives,
of someone hiding in a dark corner
behind the counter. Finally his wife
is back — his daughter is asleep on his chest.
Minutes later his tired wife is breating heavily.
He lies awake counting sirens,
listening to rats (or is someone again
trying to break in the back door).
When he finally falls asleep,
the milkman and the bread truck ring:
time to open the store.

Baltimore, Maryland 1951

Corner Myrtle and Lafayette

Invaders have beset the corner,
warrior-like thugs hanging around
undaunted, flagrantly displaying
knives, pistols, machetes; peddling
heroin, cocaine, drugs to captive
customers — blurred-eyed junkies,
who pay for their habit with
stolen welfare checks, goods in
shopping bags, not bothered by
a man who keeps vigil in a car.

The people are scared to sit on
the front porches of their houses,
afraid to let kids play outside.
They know that the harmless junkies
will, in a craze, kill for a dime
in desperation for a fix.
Myrtle and Lafayette, a landmark
for men with needle-pocked veins,
possessive drug dealers, and police
who sit in cars and wear blindness.

Every time I pass this corner
and see the numbed kids poised for a fix,
willing fools for the greedy dealers,
my heart trembles, beset with compassion
for their grieving, distressed mothers.
I feel despair, scorn for myself, for
being witness to crime and doing nothing.

I despise the man in the unmarked car
who, day after day, just sits there.
Our silence makes us accessories.

Baltimore, Maryland, March 1968

Someone Else's Dreams

Through the endless night I keep
a long, cold vigil without sleep,
from last evening till tomorrow
thinking of a thousand sorrows.
            Samuel Halkin

Attitudes change drastically
when we reach middle age;
conflicts begin to develop
between our logic and feelings,
slow down the pursuit of happiness,
the chase to reach our goal,
dreams escape with years.

Time makes us forget, or wonder,
what is good fortune all about?
Is it travel to far-away lands?
Fulfilling desires of writing?
Just being able to hold a job?
Or sitting in your yard, dreaming
you're present at a grandchild's wedding?

Snow comes to your hair, spots
of parchment cover your skin
when you reach ripened age;
your daydreams stay young, play games,
but reality confines you to your home,
eyes lose their lustiness, we read
books about someone else's dreams.

The Astronomer

To A.A.

He talks excitingly
about quasars, pulsars,
black holes in the stars.
I don't understand a word
about galaxies, planets
explorations, space discoveries.
I only know that my friend,
with a master's degree
in astronomy has big holes
in his black socks,
an empty refrigerator
and has lost six pounds
since graduation last spring.
His mind is brilliant,
he will name all the stars
in the heavens' gallery,
but sometimes he forgets
what day it is, when to pay
the phone bill, and scares
the hell out of me
by not answering the phone
a week in a row.
He is proficient in writing
on belts around Saturn,
but lacks talent to
scribble a few lines to
his mother in Florida.
He is quick to notice

new spots on the sun,
but not the spots on his shirt
which begs to be taken
for a spin to the laundry.
He gives me tips on what
phenomena in the heavens to watch,
and makes me pay the bill
and the tip in the cafeteria.

Snowstorm Blues

The heavy snowfall makes
Bel Pre Road look deserted.
My car, buried under deep snow,
resembles an igloo in the Arctic.
A raging wind, an old whistler,
howls under my windows, sounds
like the lament of a coyote.
Icicles decorate my windows,
the snowy wind smashes against
our house with furious rage.
The dimmed view of Georgia Avenue
is a white snow blanket covered
with abandoned cars, crunched
into each other in all directions.

The house is warm, pleasant;
the weatherman broadcasts more snow.
Our refrigerator is almost empty;
we have saltine crackers, a can of soup
and dried fruits in reserve.
The phone line is not working,
but thank God we have candles for
the light; the heat is off.
Frank, our student house guest,
his cheeks red, steam coming
from his nose and mouth,
tries to dig a passage
from the garage to the driveway.
But the snow keeps falling.
At night the blizzard continues.

We lie in bed in our clothes;
we shiver but we don't panic.
Suddenly we hear trucks coming.
They plow Bel Pre Road.
A police car and ambulance follow;
in the raging snowstorm the drivers
and policemen push aside the stranded cars.
Oh, I wish we had some hot coffee
for the drivers and policemen.
There is still no light, no heat.
We pray that the ambulance will reach
the endangered person in time.
Trembling I go back to bed.

Parallel

Flowers, like women,
are beautiful, complex
and dangerous.
They have strange
kinships with birds,
bats, bees, moths,
wasps and butterflies,
resembling the links
women have with
hairdressers, psycho-
analysts and other
strange creatures.
Flowers change colors,
like women their
nail polish, lipstick,
hair style and moods.
Flowers can be sweet
like the nectar
insects drink from
their bodies.
Similar to women,
their scent is pleasing,
yet their pollen
triggers tears,
hurts your throat
and disturbs your rest.
Still, we love flowers.

On a Foggy Day

A wren sits motionless
on a naked branch,
the tree looks like
an open, upward coffin
placed on a white
tablecloth, the icy mist.
I walk zigzag in the snow,
a foot deep, taking bread crumbs
for the wren that sits
unmoved on a branch.
A vast shadow of cloud
rests beneath my windows,
the whole sky falls down
and clings to the roof,
a peaceful fog hovers
over the tree in my yard,
where the wren sits
calm, cold, motionless.
I watch in silence
the heavy, gray clouds,
the bread crumbs I spread
on the yard table, and
the wren that sits unstiring
on the naked branch.
I stare with pity at
this lonely bird — the waiting
makes me sad and nervous.
Finally, the wren flies
to the table. I cannot

describe how happy I am.
But, too late . . . a squirrel
comes leaping from the woods,
and in a moment
devours the bread crumbs.
By the time I return
with more challa crust
the wren has disappeared.

On a Sunday Morning

This morning the newspaper
on my front door was missing.
But I was kissed by the sun,
caressed by a warm, fresh breeze
and greeted with songs by birds
nesting on my window casement.

I was glad the newsboy was late,
the grass had a scent of freshness
and the dew twinkled like crystal,
the squirrels were already roaming
the yard, up and down the trees
chasing each other in morning play.

I let the sun's rays embrace me
with their warmth and brilliance.
I stretched my soul to the heavens;
inwardly I said a prayer and
was thankful that the morning paper
was missing on my front door.

October 31, 1982

Fall

"Behold congenial Autumn comes,
The Sabbath of the year."

The leaves on my dogwood tree
turned red, a bleeding color,
like the evening sun in the sky.

The dying leaves are strewn
over the grass; they remind me
of life's twilight; how years die.

How our hair changes colors,
how our longings dissolve gently —
melt in the splendor of fall.

I know my dogwood tree will bloom,
new leaves will blossom in spring,
birds will dwell on her branches.

The marigolds, violets and lilies,
like in the past springs and summers,
will not flourish until next fall.

Will I be still here to see
the roses bursting, the tulips. Will I
hear the voice of birds and the bees?

But spring is far away, a long wait,
clouds, ice, wind and snow must pass,
before my dogwood tree will bloom.

Let's celebrate the festival of fall.
There is beauty in the golden leaves.

For Further Reading

❖ ❖ ❖

GENERAL

Nathan and Maryann Ausubel, editors. *A Treasury of Jewish Poetry*. New York: Crown Publishers, Inc., 1957.

Israel Ch. Biletzky. *Essays on Yiddish Poetry and Prose Writers*. Tel Aviv: I.L. Peretz Library, 1969.

Syzmon Dubnow. *Weltgeschichte des Judischen Wolkes, Volume II-IV*.

Helena Frank. *Yiddish Tales*. Philadelphia: The Jewish Publication Society of America, 1912.

General Encyclopedia in Yiddish. YIDN-VI. New York: Jewish Encyclopedia Handbook, Inc., 1964.

Benjamin and Barbara Harshav. *American Yiddish Poetry: A Bilingual Anthology*. Berkeley: University of California Press, 1986.

Irving Howe. *World of Our Fathers*. New York: Simon and Schuster, 1976.

Irving Howe and Eliezer Greenberg. *Voices from the Yiddish*. New York: Schocken Book, 1975.

Israel Knox. *The World of Yiddish*. New York: Hebrew Publishing Company, 1947.

A. Anatoli Kuznetzov. *Babi Yar*. New York: Farrar, Straus and Giroux, 1970.

Charles Madison. *Yiddish Literature: Its Scope and Major Writers*. New York: Schocken Books, 1968.

Nachman Maisel. *Zurickbliken in Perespektivn*. Tel Aviv: Peretz Publishing Company, 1962.

S. Niger. "Yiddish Literature from the midst of the 18th Century until 1942," *Algemeine Encyclopedie in Yiddish*, vol. iii, pp. 650174. New York: Central Yiddish Culture Organization, 1948.

Powstanie W. *Ghetcie Warszawskim 1943 R*. Warsaw: Government Publishing House, 1945.

Ernest Rena. Introduction to *Histoire du peuple d'Israel*.

Elias Tcherikower. *Jewish Martyrology and Jewish Historiography*, Yivo, Bleter XVII, 1941, Yivo Annual of Jewish Social Science, Vol. I, 1946.

Aharon Vinkovetzky, Abba Kovner and Sinai Lechter. *Anthology of Yiddish Folksongs*. Jerusalem: Mount Scopus Publications, Magnes Press, 1987.

Uriel Weinreich. *College Yiddish*. New York: Yivo Institute for Jewish Research, 1949.

MENDELE MOCHER SFORIM

Klein Mendele. *Selections from the Writing of Mendele Mocher Sforim*. Edited and published by Joseph Kaits (Kutzenogy). New York, 1931 (Yiddish).

Kol Kitve. *Mendele Mocher Sfarim* (Hebrew). Tel Aviv, 1947.

Ruth R. Wisse. *A Shtetl and Other Yiddish Novellas of Bygone Days*

(Shloyme Reb Chayims) Mendele the Bookpeddler. New York: The Library of Jewish Studies: Behrman House, 1973.

SHOLOM ALEICHEM

Sholom Aleichem, *"Di Gas" (The Street)*. Dialogue translated by Dan Miron. Ale werk, I, pp. 476-477.

"Shalom Aleichem," *Encyclopedia Judaica*, vol. 14, pp. 1272-1286.

Shalom Aleichem: Ale werk fun Sholem Aleykehm. Translated by Dan Miron, Folksfond oysgabe 1917-1925, vol 5, pp. 9-109.

Dan Miron. *Sholem Aleykhem: Person, Persona, Presence*. Yivo Institute of Jewish Research, 1942.

Maurice Samuel. *The World of Sholom Aleichem*. New York: Knopf, 1943.

YITZHOK LEIBUSH PERETZ

Jacob Glatshtein. "Peretz and the Jewish Nineteenth Century," *Voices from the Yiddish: Essays, Memoirs, Diaries*. Edited by Irving Howe and Eliezer Greenberg. New York: Schocken Books, 1975.

Sol Liptzin. *Stories from Peretz*. New York: Hebrew Publishing Company, 1947.

Y.L. Peretz. *Essays of Y.L. Peretz*. New York: Yivo Institute for Jewish Research, 1939.

Nahum Socolow. *Perzenlechkeiten* (Personalities). Buenos Aires: The Central Committee of Polish Jewry in Argentina, 1948.

ISRAEL JOSHUA SINGER

I.J. Singer. "Fun A Welt Vos Iz Nishto Mer." (Yiddish) New York: Matones, 1946.

I.J. Singer. *Yoshe Kalb*. New York: Harper & Row, 1965.

I.J. Singer. *The Brothers Ashkenazi*. Translated by Maurice Samuel. Cleveland, Ohio: Forum Books, 1963 (originally published in 1936).

ISSAC BASHEVIS SINGER

Isaac Bashevis Singer. *The Family Moskat*. New York: Farrar Straus and Giroux, 1952.

Paul Kresh. *I.B. Singer: The Magician of West 86th Street*. New York: The Dial Press, 1979.

CHAIM GRADE

James Cohen. "Chaim Grade — A Great Yiddish Writer of the Century." United Jewish Federation Virginia News, February 7, 1987.

Chaim Grade. "Longing" (poem), translated by Inna Hecker. Midstream, June-July 1987.

Chaim Grade. *My Mother's Sabbath Days: A Memoir*. Translated by Chaina Kleinerman-Goldstein and Inna Hecker. New York: Alfred A. Knopf, 1980.

Chaim Grade. *Shain Fun Farloirene Shtern*. Buenos Aires: Central Committee of Polish Jews in Argentina, 1950.

AARON ZEITLIN

Albert H. Friedlander. *Out of the Whirlwind*. Philadelphia: Jew Publication Society of America, 1978.

H. LEIVICK

H. Leivick. *Mit Der Shaarit Hapleita* (With the Remnants of the Holocaust). New York: Cico Publishing House, 1948.

H. Leivick. *Of Czarisher Katorge*. Tel Aviv: I.L. Peretz Library, 1959.

H. Leivick. Oisgeklibene *Schriften Poesia, Theatro, Ensayos Ateneo Literario* — IWO. Buenos Aires, 1969.

Emma Schreiver. *Mit Zenen Do!* (We Are Here). Detroit: Itzchok and Mendele Foundation, 1948.

GLUECKEL OF HAMELN

B.Z. Abraham. *Life of Glueckel of Hameln*. New York: Yiddish Welt, 1962.

Glueckel of Hameln, *Encyclopedia Judaica,* vol vii, pp. 629-620.

Szymon Dubnow. *Die Welt-Geschichte Fun Yiddishn Folk,* vol. ii. Buenos Aires, 1953.

Yivo. *Bleter,* vol vi, pp. 183-144, 1934.

S. Niger. Die Yiddishe Literatur *un die Lezern Der Pinkas*. Wilno, 1912.

Samuel Rozansky. *Literature Idish-Vida I Toms, Ateneo Literario En El IWO*. Buenos Aires, 1973.

ABRAHAM SUTZKEVER

Di Goldene Keit. Number 128. Tel Aviv, 1990.

Melodies and Colors in the Sutzkever Symphony. Of Three Worlds Anthology, Buenos Aires, 1953.

Yaakov Tvi Schargel. "Mit Fulle Emers." Tel Aviv: Israel Books, 1990.

Sarah Zweig Betsky. *Onions and Cucumbers and Plums*. Detroit: Wayne State University Press, 1989.

VASSILY GROSSMAN

Jacob Frumkin, Gregor Aronson, Alexis Goldenweiser and Joseph Lewitan, editors. *Russian Jewry, 1917-1967*. New York: Thomas Yoseloff, 1969.

Vassily Grossman. *Life and Fate*. New York: Harper and Row, 1987.

Khone Shmeruk, editor. *A Shpigl Oyf A Shteyn: An Anthology of Poetry and Prose by Twelve Soviet Yiddish Writers, selected by B. Hrushowski, K. Shmeruk and A. Sutzkever*. Tel Aviv: Di Goldene Keyt, I.L. Peretz Publishing House, 1964.

Judd L. Teller. *The Kremlin, the Jews and the Middle East*. Syracuse, 1957.

About the Author

Since he arrived in the United States in 1947, Herman Taube has written for numbers of newspapers, including the *Jewish Daily Forward* and *The Jewish Week* (Washington, D.C.), and the *Algemeiner Journal* (Brooklyn, New York), and *On Hoyb* (Miami). He has written numbers of books, the most recent *Land of Blue Skies* and *Between the Shadows: New & Selected Works*. A graduate of American University with an M.A. in Literature-Creative Writing, he lectures regularly on Yiddish Literature, World War II and the Holocaust. He has taught at the University of Maryland and The American University and is currently a faculty member at the College of Jewish Studies — Board of Jewish Education. At present, he is White House correspondent for the *Jewish Forward*.